Letting Student Voices Shine

This book provides clear, accessible strategies for developing your students' public speaking abilities – a valuable skill to help your students shine.

Letting Student Voices Shine provides a clear curriculum for improving public speaking competencies, including a progression of mastery, implementable classroom activities, video demonstrations, and rubrics for helping teachers to evaluate and students to improve. In addition to instructional and example videos created specifically for this book, chapters also feature TED Talk examples – the gold standard for effectively conveying accurate, easy-to-understand information to a target audience – to illustrate key points on what does or doesn't work, and why.

Whether used as is, or broken up to focus on specific public speaking skills, teachers in any subject area will find this book an invaluable tool to ease students into public speaking until they are expert orators.

Todd Stanley is the author of over 20 teacher education books, including *A Teacher's Toolbox for Gifted Education: 20 Strategies You Can Use Today to Challenge Gifted Students*. He has been an educator for over 28 years and is the Gifted Services Coordinator for Pickerington Schools, as well as an Adjunct Professor teaching gifted education at the University of Cincinnati.

Letting Student Voices Shine

Using Online Talks to Teach Public Speaking

Todd Stanley

Routledge
Taylor & Francis Group
NEW YORK AND LONDON

Designed cover image: Getty Images

First published 2025
by Routledge
605 Third Avenue, New York, NY 10158

and by Routledge
4 Park Square, Milton Park, Abingdon, Oxon, OX14 4RN

Routledge is an imprint of the Taylor & Francis Group, an informa business

© 2025 Todd Stanley

The right of Todd Stanley to be identified as author of this work has been asserted in accordance with sections 77 and 78 of the Copyright, Designs and Patents Act 1988.

All rights reserved. No part of this book may be reprinted or reproduced or utilised in any form or by any electronic, mechanical, or other means, now known or hereafter invented, including photocopying and recording, or in any information storage or retrieval system, without permission in writing from the publishers.

Trademark notice: Product or corporate names may be trademarks or registered trademarks, and are used only for identification and explanation without intent to infringe.

ISBN: 978-1-032-47408-3 (hbk)
ISBN: 978-1-032-47023-8 (pbk)
ISBN: 978-1-003-38598-1 (ebk)
ISBN: 978-1-003-60020-6 (ebk+)

DOI: 10.4324/9781003385981

Typeset in Palatino
by Deanta Global Publishing Services, Chennai, India

All supplemental online resources mentioned in this book can be found here:

https://www.thegiftedguy.com/public-speaking

Contents

Introduction – Why public speaking is important: By Verlin Zhang, 7th grade student from a DDC Public Speaking course 1

1 Why you should teach your students how to publicly speak 7

2 What is a TED Talk and why should you use them to teach students about public speaking 18

3 Creating a safe space 28

4 How to get started – the two-minute bio speech 39

5 Finding your voice 53

6 Expository – the five-minute TED-Ed speech 72

7 Demonstrative – the ten-minute speech 90

8 Persuasive – the 15-minute speech 110

9 Oratorical – the 20-minute TED Talk 134

10 The little things matter 158

Conclusion: How students can continue to build their confidence in public speaking 171

Appendix *177*
Works cited *178*

Introduction – Why public speaking is important

By Verlin Zhang, 7th grade student from a DDC Public Speaking course

A girl is standing in the middle of the theater while what feels like a million eyes are staring at her. A spotlight shines on her in the middle of the stage presenting her like an angel, but she feels none of the confidence of such a holy creature. Instead, she has wobbly legs, shaking arms with goosebumps, and eyes that don't know where to look. Her palms and face are sweating as if she just finished a two-hour training session of tennis. She is here to deliver a message about the student council, but when she opens her mouth her voice quivers like she has grabbed an exposed wire and is being shocked. The audience can't make sense of what she is talking about. They can only hear squeaky and shaky words spill out of her mouth as if she were a mouse. Even though she is 12, she feels like a toddler who experiences everything around her in an awkward manner, questioning herself about where she is and who she is. Can you guess who this girl is?

It is me, a teenage girl from China who has no confidence in speaking in public but has been asked to do so, even though I have never been taught how to do this. I have learned algebra, how to analyze a character from a literary work, and how matter works. Of course, I have never needed to use any of these in my real life. And yet, here I found myself needing a skill and not having been taught it in a proper manner. If you ever wondered why public speaking is so important, this is a perfect example. People find themselves in situations where they have to speak publicly every single day. It might be in school when the teacher calls on you to answer a question. Or at a restaurant when the waitress asks you what you want from the menu and you need to communicate exactly how you want your food. It could be when your mom wants to shop and then eat, but you are starving and want to convince her to eat then shop. If you have ever wondered why people should even bother to learn public speaking, here are three reasons why I think this is such a valuable skill.

Public speaking can be very useful throughout life by helping students gain more confidence. It can also make you feel more comfortable with people in general. According to a study by North Carolina Cooperative Extension, all of the participants who took part in public speaking programs reported that it increased their confidence. When you are confident, more people will believe what you say, even if you do not believe it yourself. Another example of how gaining confidence helps students, which occurs almost every day, is that they will be more willing to speak up and participate in class. When you are participating more in class, the teacher sees that you are learning the material better and you get verification that you understand it as well. It could also improve critical thinking because students are more willing to share their opinions and back them up if they feel confident in them. Something I noticed about myself was a massive change between two speeches, one in 4th grade and the other in 6th. In my 4th-grade speech, I felt my palms sweating, legs shaking, wobbly hands, and a frightened face when speaking to people in my class, even though there were only 17 of them. I was scared to say something wrong because I thought people might laugh and make jokes about me. Because of that, I kept saying *umms* and *likes*, which caused my speech to be not so satisfying to listen to. Not only that, people were confused about what on earth I wanted to communicate to them. I looked like an outsider who does not know what I am doing here and what to say. That is when I felt that I did not have the confidence to speak in public, so I started to take public speaking classes. Two years later, I presented a speech like I was having a conversation with the audience, looking very relaxed and confident on stage. I used more body language to better express my feelings and thoughts for the audience to understand. I spoke more fluently with fewer *umms* and *likes*, which provided a flow for the whole speech while making it sound more professional. As you can see, there is a big difference between the two speeches before and after learning public speaking. If gaining more confidence will not convince you, here is another reason.

Learning public speaking can also help you to organize your thoughts better, which makes you speak more fluently. Having a clear plan of what you will say in your mind can make people understand you better. It can also be a way of showing that you have confidence when speaking. You will start to speak fluently with good body language and posture, and have more interactions with the audience. When people are nervous and scared, they tend to doubt themselves. You will start to lose faith in what you are trying to communicate, and this lack of confidence will reflect in your speech, such as having awkward pauses for thinking. But when you know what you are supposed to say and you speak fluently, people will believe you are more professional.

When I first learned public speaking, during my first speech I presented, I was twisting my tongue deciding which words to use to express what I wanted to say. I mumbled a lot and I spoke in a soft voice that only cats could hear. I was confused and struggled with my own choice of words. This might have caused the audience to think I did not have a clear structure in my head of what I was going to present, which caused me to lose credibility as a speaker. Also, because I was struggling with my structure, I would say whatever came to mind at that second.

For example, I was giving a speech on how dogs are different from cats. I finished one slide of information and moved on to the next. But suddenly, I forgot I needed to add another fact from the last slide. So I interrupted my own speech by saying, "Now I will talk about why cats are easier to raise than a dog … Oh, and something to add to the last slide, dogs have a better sense of smell than cats". It is not organized and makes the audience think I do not know what I am talking about. The audience will also feel like they are riding on a mental rollercoaster, going up and down with my ever-changing topics. By learning how to organize my thoughts better, I can state all examples in each topic, making every word effective and useful for my entire speech.

Another example of why it is important for someone to have a clear idea in their mind of what they are going to communicate is when a student raises their hand to answer a question or the teacher calls on them. If they are unsure of how to begin, they may start to say *umms*, *likes*, and talking while thinking about what to say next. This will confuse the teacher and other students about what he/she is talking about. By learning public speaking, they can have a better idea of what to say. With a clear structure, they will impress their teachers and classmates.

Learning public speaking can help one improve their organization of words and thinking. Organizing your thoughts can make you speak more fluently, help you to speak with more confidence, and make people think you are more professional. It can help in real-life situations, such as when you are in a class and asked to answer a question orally. This leads us to our final reason why public speaking is especially important: it is a skill you will use very often throughout life.

The last reason why public speaking is important is that it will be used often in your adult life, not just in school. It can be used when communicating with your family, when you are interviewing for a job or doing business, or in your daily interactions with people. It can be used in many situations when you are an adult.

In my family, we also have times when we use public speaking. For example, when we have important discussions or host a banquet with our big family, we tend to do some public speaking by thanking each other. There is also an expert in my family, who is my aunt, who has been learning public speaking for over ten years. She has gained lots of confidence in her posture, words, and the structure of her ideas when speaking. I often learn from chatting with her. One thing I learn is how to communicate clearly because she builds up layers of evidence that help people understand more of what she is saying. This is the skill that I am missing when I am convincing people, as sometimes I fight with my own words. This is also how every time when I have a disagreement with her, she is able to convince me that I don't understand why I would ever think that way. She is a great example of why learning public speaking is useful and important, especially in family situations. I hope one day to be the expert in my family, just like my aunt.

Learning public speaking can help in the business world when you are presenting information to individuals or a group. My aunt works for a big company in China. I was shocked because it was tough to get into this company, so I asked her what made her appealing to them. She answered that it was probably because of her fantastic skills in presenting herself to the company. This is something that would be important for anyone in the business world because most people don't communicate very effectively. If you are someone who communicates well through your public speaking, this will give you more opportunities for jobs and to give people a more positive first impression, which can help with future business. But on the other hand, if you aren't very skilled in public speaking, you might not have as many chances as those who are good at public speaking. That is why public speaking is important in the business world.

Lastly, public speaking can be used in our daily lives too. For example, when my mom goes to the bank and communicates with people about her credit card or other business-related matters, she needs to use public speaking to let them know what she wants. If you don't know how to say something clearly enough for others to understand, then how are you supposed to know that they are doing the things that you want or need them to do? Sometimes simple requests like that are not that easy to do when you don't know how to express yourself, and that is where public speaking is important.

Any one of these skills would be good for an adult to have, but with public speaking, you can have all three of them. Being an adult can be difficult as it is, which is why having the confidence to communicate with others will make it a little easier.

I have shown you many reasons why public speaking is extremely important and useful. Public speaking is used every single day. It can make you more confident and comfortable when speaking in public or at school. You can even get your way more often. Most importantly, it can better help you with communication.

Public speaking is also very useful in the business world. Having better public speaking skills can win more opportunities from companies, and it is also a strength compared to others. Public speaking will be used in your daily life as well. From going to the bank, to buying things at the grocery store, to ordering food at a restaurant, you will be faced with having to speak in public every day.

Hopefully I have convinced you that public speaking is very important. Now is the time to move on to the next stage, which is how. How can someone become a better public speaker? There will be lots of tips and strategies that can be used to improve and practice this skill. Keep exploring how to become a great public speaker throughout the book.

1

Why you should teach your students how to publicly speak

The comedian Jerry Seinfeld once said,

> According to most studies, people's number one fear is public speaking. Number two is death. Death is number two. Does that sound right? This means to the average person, if you go to a funeral, you're better off in the casket than doing the eulogy.

As funny as this is, it is true. When asked what their biggest fear is, most people will put public speaking above death, spiders, heights, and flying. Keep in mind, no one has died from public speaking (unless you want to count President William Henry Harrison, who spoke for 8,445 words at his inauguration in the pouring rain and died of pneumonia a month later).

Three out of four people suffer from some form of speech anxiety. Now keep in mind, this doesn't mean they are terrified of it to the point of not being able to function. This simply means they get really nervous when having to speak in front of others. It would be the difference between someone who is afraid of flying but still sucks it up and powers through it when they need to travel somewhere, and someone who is so fearful of flying that they are unable to bring themselves to step onboard. John

DOI: 10.4324/9781003385981-2

Madden, the football announcer, became so afraid of flying that even though his responsibilities required him to travel all across the United States, he did so in a giant RV instead. There is a name for those who are afraid of public speaking: glossophobia. It is a form of social anxiety disorder (SAD).

So what's the big deal? If you are afraid of flying, you simply don't get on airplanes. If you are afraid of heights, you avoid tall structures. If you are afraid of public speaking, you simply avoid situations where you might have to speak in public, right? Unfortunately, it is not so easy. There are times in one's life where there is no avoiding speaking in public. There are simply situations where having this skill is not only going to come in handy, it is going to be greatly beneficial. Because it comes with an advantage, the inability to speak can be a disadvantage. This could be in continuing education, a job, or even in one's social life.

A person will need the skill throughout his education. There are various ways to communicate what have been learned in a class, and oral communication is a fairly important one. This could be having the courage to speak when called on by the teacher, taking part in a discussion, or the defense of a dissertation. Being able to express what has been learned in spoken form shows the teacher an understanding.

If somebody thinks he can go through school avoiding having to speak in public, he might be surprised to learn that the fear of public speaking can cause a 10% impairment in college graduation. With some courses requiring class participation, students would rather fail quietly than have to speak in front of their peers. This dread of speaking in public is so prevalent that even though they work really hard to get into college and get their work done, this fear is stronger.

This need for public speaking does not end when students finish schooling. It follows them into their professional lives. The inability to speak competently in public can literally cost upwards of 10% of wages as those with the skill advance. Moving up the corporate ladder can also take a hit as it has a 15% impairment on people's ability to obtain managerial and leadership positions. Why is this? Because leaders can publicly speak.

When they asked businesses what skills they were most looking for from graduate students entering the workforce, the number one skill was not business knowledge, technology, or innovation. The top skill was oral communication (Figure 1.1).

Presentation skills were also in the top tier of skills sought by employers, and communication in general was the most coveted proficiency.

Even without the statistics, just use common sense. The better one can speak in public, the better the chances are of getting hired and moving up the ranks. And yet only 8% of the population takes the necessary steps to help with this problem. Think of the advantage this gives this small group of the population

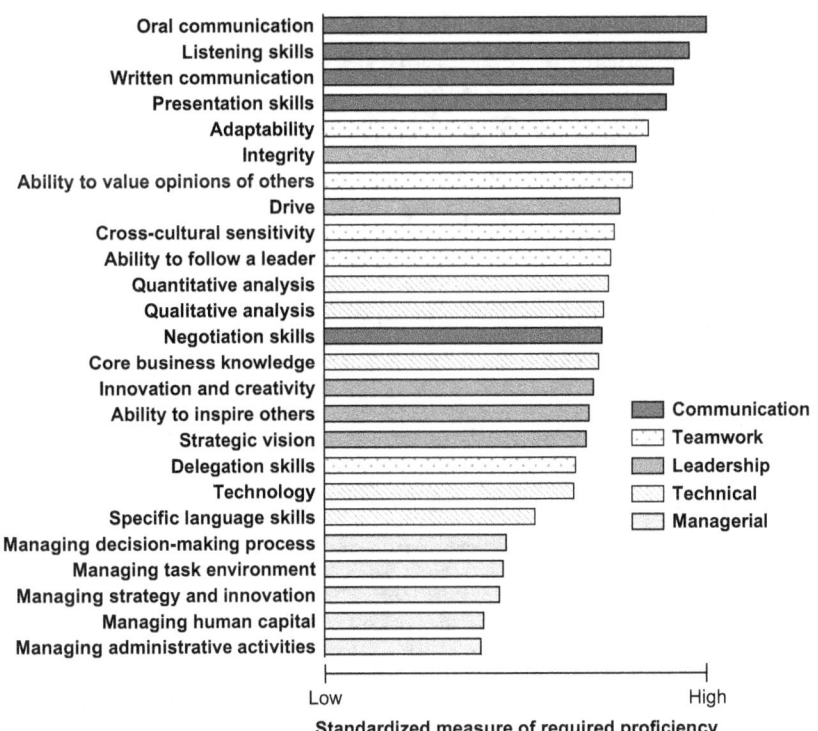

FIGURE 1.1

over the majority who are either scared of speaking in public or are unwilling to become better at it. Think of the advantage you could give your students by focusing on this very skill in your classroom.

Survival skills

Tony Wagner developed a list of survival skills in his book *The Global Achievement Gap* following interviews with many top business leaders and observations of hundreds of American classrooms. He discovered a vast difference between the skills businesses seek and expect and the skills students are being taught in school. The survival skills the corporate world were looking for were:

- Critical Thinking and Problem-solving
- Collaboration Across Networks
- Agility and Adaptability
- Initiative and Entrepreneurialism
- Accessing and Analyzing Information
- Curiosity and Imagination
- Effective Oral and Written Communication

These survival skills are very timely right now because people can find most information at a moment's notice. Because of this, there is less of a need to spend time in school memorizing content. We should be using this time to teach students skills that prepare them not for jobs tomorrow, but for jobs five to ten years down the road – jobs that do not yet exist.

One of these skills is effective oral communication. Why is this one of the sought-after skills? Because you could have the best idea in the world but if you can't communicate it to others, it doesn't matter. Thomas Edison was not just one of the best inventors of the early 20th century, he was also one of the best communicators about his inventions. This is what made him the legend he is. Steve Jobs was a master at communicating what his company sold, which was not products, but ideas. Sojourner Truth is not just a symbol for the rights of African-Americans post-Civil War; she advocated with her voice at the Women's Convention in Akron, Ohio, in 1851.

When you look at some of the most influential leaders of all time, the list goes something like this:

- John F. Kennedy
- Martin Luther King Jr.
- Winston Churchill
- Abraham Lincoln
- Nelson Mandela
- Gandhi
- Margaret Thatcher
- Franklin Roosevelt
- Ruth Bader Ginsburg
- Socrates

What do all of these leaders have in common? They said things that are remembered for hundreds, if not thousands, of years in the case of Socrates. If you don't believe me, take a gander at some of the quotes attributed to each of them:

- John F. Kennedy – *Ask not what your country can do for you, but what you can do for your country*
- Martin Luther King Jr. – *I have a dream*
- Winston Churchill – *Attitude is a little thing that makes a big difference*
- Abraham Lincoln – *A house divided against itself cannot stand*
- Nelson Mandela – *What counts in life is not the mere fact that we have lived. It is what difference we have made to the lives of others*
- Gandhi – *You must be the change you wish to see in the world*
- Margaret Thatcher – *If you want something said, ask a man; if you want something done, ask a woman*
- Franklin Roosevelt – *The only thing we have to fear is fear itself*

- ♦ Ruth Bader Ginsburg – *Real change, enduring change, happens one step at a time*
- ♦ Socrates – *An unexamined life is not worth living*

Keep in mind, they said these things. They did not write these things. These legendary quotes were spoken. And because they were spoken, they are that much more powerful.

Take the first quote here, "Ask not what your country can do for you, but what you can do for your country". As written, it seems very wise. But when it is spoken, it is so much more weighty. You can experience this for yourself by watching this clip: https://www.youtube.com/watch?v=P1PbQlVMp98. Even Socrates, who we unfortunately do not have recordings of, made a living at public speaking. He would speak to his students and share his wisdom with them. In fact, Socrates did not write any of his dialogues down – they were transcribed by others.

The lesson is, if you have something important to communicate, the best way to do so is by saying it aloud to others. And in current times, where everything is recorded, people can expand their audience to more than just those in the room. Sir Ken Robinson, who spoke about creativity in schools, had nearly 1,000 people in the auditorium listening to him. But since his recording was posted on the internet through TED.com, it has been viewed more than 75 million times.

The tagline of the TED company is "ideas worth spreading". If students have an idea they want to spread, they have to be willing to put themselves out there and tell it to others.

Some of the advantages of learning to speak in public

By choosing to purposefully teach your students public speaking skills, you are doing more than simply teaching them how to speak in public. You are also teaching them:

1. Critical thinking – the definition of this is one's ability to objectively analyze and evaluate an issue so that a judgment can be formed. In other words, teaching people to think for

themselves. This is the ultimate goal of teaching, not for students to memorize facts or to recite information as it is given to them. The purpose of teaching is for students to be able to make something of this information for themselves and to create something original. We want to produce thinkers, and public speaking requires one to not just recite memorized words, but to understand them in such a way that they can be communicated to others.

2. Improved communication skills – when students develop their speeches, they have to determine the best way to communicate their ideas to their audience. This is, of course, easier said than done. Just because they understand it does not mean they can explain it to someone else so that it can be understood. When someone is giving a speech, whatever idea is trying to be conveyed must be done in a language that the audience can understand. This does not mean speaking their native tongue. This means putting it in terms, phrases, and groupings that the audience can digest and get a clear understanding. One will learn very quickly that the key to this is using details to make the communication clear. Once this is mastered this will carry over into day-to-day communication with people.

3. Persuasion – even though speeches might vary in the amount of persuading, nearly all are trying to persuade in some fashion. Persuading that it is worth listening to, persuading that the idea has merit, persuading someone to think about something in a whole new light, and the ultimate persuasion is for those listening to change their minds. The speaker knowing how to craft the words and message in such a way as to have people want to be persuaded is a valuable superpower. Let's be frank, it allows one to get one's way a whole lot more. This might be something as simple as deciding where to eat tonight or something with weight such as whether to buy this particular house or not. This power of persuasion is also beneficial in the working world, whether trying to convince someone to buy something, use something, or believe in something.

4. Leadership skills – leadership is one of those skills that everyone sees value in but not a lot of people know how to teach.

The reason being it is like public speaking; reading about it in a book or watching someone demonstrate it in a YouTube video isn't going to do the trick. You actually have to do it. In order to teach leadership, students need to be put into positions where they can demonstrate leadership skills. This does not necessarily mean running for student council or being an officer in the National Honor Society chapter. It could be something as simple as taking on a leadership role in a group project or stepping up when the teacher asks for volunteers. Many times the best place to display leadership is on the sports field. Leaders emerge naturally from team sports. One way to teach leadership in the classroom, though, is through public speaking. First and foremost a leader is not afraid to speak. Someone can have a great idea, but if that person is not willing to tell others about it, that idea will die on the vine. You, as the teacher, have to give students the confidence to be leaders if they are going to lead. Public speaking provides this confidence.

5. Civil discourse – there are many people who know how to argue, but very few who know how to conduct civil discourse. The difference is that in an argument, you are rarely listening to the other side or listening to learn. You are speaking to make your point. Civil discourse, on the other hand, has one listening just as much as one is speaking. Students can learn a lot from what others have to say. A successful debate is not one where one side defeats another, but one where both sides learn from the other's perspective. It might not change their mind but it gives them a little more information toward understanding. Even though most of the speeches talked about in this book do not involve a back and forth, public speaking can lead to formal debate, either in class or in academic extra-curricular clubs such as Speech and Debate, Model United Nations, or Youth and Government.

6. Personal growth – personal growth is the ability to learn skills that will have a positive impact on a student's life and increase their overall well-being. Being able to speak in public does require courage. Their ability to adapt to this fear and to put their nerves aside shows a tremendous amount of

personal growth. They set a goal, they work toward that goal, and they accomplish that goal. That's how people grow, and that's how people learn to become better public speakers.

7. Performance skills – public speaking is equal parts substance and style. Having very important things to share with an audience is one thing, but if they aren't interested in how it is being said, or they lack confidence in the speaker, or if they simply don't like the person, then the idea will die in committee. Words are very important, but the style in which these words are delivered is equally if not more important. Many a politician with great ideas was not able to rise up the ranks because they did not convince people through their style that their ideas were worth listening to (I'm looking at you, Al Gore).

8. Developed vocabulary and fluency – the spoken word and the written word can often be very different from each other. But they both have to have rhythm and flow in order for people to understand what is being said. This means using appropriate words that convey an idea clearly and, more importantly, give the audience an image of what is being talked about.

9. How to be a better observer – when you become a public speaker, it allows you to gain an appreciation for others who also speak publicly because you know how difficult it is to do. There will be several examples of TED Talks to watch in this book that will teach things speakers ought to do and those that will show you what not to do. It does require listening carefully not only to the spoken words but also looking at the non-verbals, which can communicate the opposite of what is trying to be communicated. Watching others speak makes you want to listen better so that you can steal and learn from what they do.

10. Confidence – probably the most important advantage of all. Everyone is capable of speaking in public. Everyone has something to say. But only a select few actually do this. The difference is they possess the confidence to get in front of others and care more about their message than how people are going to judge them. You want to teach students that if they have something important they want to share with others,

they need to be confident enough to do so. They need to have confidence in their ideas and message. Unfortunately the only way they are going to gain this confidence is by actually speaking in public. But you can guarantee them that the more they do it, the more experience they gain and the more confident they will become. It doesn't become any easier. They simply get better at it.

Giving students voice

One of the most important advantages of public speaking is that it gives your students voice. Everyone has an opinion that has value in being shared, but needs to have the means to do so. The world is full of great ideas that never saw the light of day because the person with the idea was unable to convey it to others.

Part of the confidence you will instill in your students will be the self-assurance to share their ideas with others in effective ways because kids have important ideas too. Sometimes they even have better ideas if they are given the space and opportunity to share them.

By giving your students voice, it allows them to shine. It also allows you and others to learn from them.

> **TED TALK**
>
> An example of a TED talk that explains the importance of student voice: *What Adults Can Learn from Kids* by Adora Svitak.

Shining a spotlight

Ultimately what it comes down to is this: you will teach your students a lot of things that they are going to forget. They forget these things not because they do not see value in what they are learning, nor is it because you did not teach it to them well. The reason why most students forget what you have taught them is that they are not exposed to it in their daily lives. How many times does the *Magna Carta* come up in everyday conversation, or how often does one need to solve irrational numbers?

However, public speaking is a skill that people will experience in their everyday lives. Those who possess this skill have a clear advantage over those who do not. It is never a skill that will go underutilized. Anyone who wishes to will have ample opportunity to use this skill and to hone it. As a public school teacher, I have been developing my public speaking skills for the past 30 years and am still am learning things each and every time I speak. Like playing a sport, public speaking is not a skill one ever gains complete mastery of. There is always room to get better.

This ability to speak in public will lead your students to opportunities that those who lack the ability will miss out on. It is a clear advantage that will lead them to greater success in education, their careers, and even their personal lives.

> **TODD TALK**
>
> To watch a video explaining the value of public speaking that can be shown to students, go to: https://youtu.be/P8mtycKVtls
>
>

# 2

What is a TED Talk and why should you use them to teach students about public speaking

TED originally started as a small technology conference in 1984 where really smart folks tried to explain something complicated so that people who were not experts could understand. As it continued to grow, it expanded to entertainment and design, thus the acronym TED (technology, entertainment, and design). As the internet expanded its reach, the speeches began to be recorded and put online. First posted in 2006, these were deemed TED Talks, which people could view for free on the website www.ted.com. Suddenly, instead of having thousands of people watch these speeches, the audience expanded to millions.

TED has now has become so much more than just a conference. It has become a place where people can share their passions and expertise in a way that resonates and connects with others. There are TED Talks that will move you to tears, some that will make your jaw drop, and others that will make you want to go out and change the world. Most important for your journey in teaching public speaking, it is a vast resource of speeches that can be used to help your students. It provides the outline to use for their speeches, gives you exemplars to show students what it looks like when it is working, and sometimes even what it looks like when it is not.

DOI: 10.4324/9781003385981-3

What is the purpose of a TED Talk?

The tagline for TED is "ideas worth spreading". This sums up pretty well what the purpose of a TED Talk is, which is to tell the viewers about an interesting idea that they can relate to and understand, even though they originally might not have found it interesting or pertinent. In order to do this, the speakers have to present in the language of the audience in order for them to understand. What this means is that when physicists speak to other physicists, they use a language they commonly understand, but that someone who is not a physicist might not be able to decipher. This is what is known as the language of the discipline. Certain disciplines, let's use the example of a teacher since you speak that language, use language that is common for others in that discipline, but unfamiliar to those who are not. So I can say to use formative assessments with your students learning about public speaking and to evaluate for mastery and you would know what the heck I am talking about. Others not in education might not have the slightest idea of what a formative assessment is, and they might also not know what determining mastery looks like.

The brilliant thing that TED does is make really smart people talk in a way that people not as smart as them can comprehend. This is the purpose of nearly every speech, whether a TED Talk or a teacher presenting a lesson on commas. You are the person with the information, and you are delivering it to people who do not have it. You have to explain it under the assumption that they do not know your language so that you can reach everyone in the audience. TED Talks do an excellent job of showing how this is done and how it is not about sounding smart but about being understood. It is all about clear communication.

Finding just the right length

TED Talks run at various lengths. There are some that are as short as three minutes, while some are ten minutes in length. When the conference first began, like many conferences, the average speech was 90 minutes in length. After a few years of doing this, the organizers of TED realized that quality was more important than quantity. A 1995 study by the United States Navy found that 20 minutes for a speech was equivalent to a 50-minute speech in regard to information learned, so why not simply make the speech shorter and save everyone the time? Forcing a speaker to tell what they know in a quarter of the time makes the speakers more efficient. All of the fat is cut from the speech and all that is left is the prime rib. Speakers have to stay laser-focused, meaning the audience is only getting the good stuff.

Not only that, as they began to launch these talks on the internet in 2006, the talks needed to have a length that people could watch during a small break. Asking folks to sit down and watch a movie-length speech is a big ask. Asking them for 15 to 20 minutes of their time is more palatable. As a result, the longest a TED Talk is supposed to run is 18–20 minutes. This is the sweet spot according to TED because this is how long the human mind can pay attention.

Chris Anderson, who is the current curator of TED, explained its length as follows:

> It [18 minutes] is long enough to be serious and short enough to hold people's attention ... The 18-minute length also works much like the way Twitter forces people to be disciplined in what they write. By forcing speakers who are used to going on for 45 minutes to bring it down to 18, you get them to really think about what they want to say. What is the key point they want to communicate? It has a clarifying effect. It brings discipline.
>
> (Gallo, 2014)

In other words, this format prevents people from being windbags.

And this is the appropriate length for students learning how to give a speech. It is short enough that they can accomplish it but not intimidate them. An 18-minute speech is a bit of a challenge, but it is not impossible.

It also teaches students the power of brevity and that the more one talks, the less people hear. If they want the audience to remember the significant things that were said, the audience still needs to be paying attention when they say it.

Some of the most important speeches in the last century were not of great length. Here are some examples of speeches that were around 18 minutes in length:

- ♦ Martin Luther King Jr. – I Have a Dream (17 minutes)
- ♦ John F. Kennedy – Rice University Space Race (19 minutes)
- ♦ Steve Jobs – Stay Hungry, Stay Foolish (15 minutes)
- ♦ Malala Yousafzai – Speech to the United Nations (18 minutes)

Too many people think it is about the quantity of what is said, but history has shown it is the quality. Abraham Lincoln's Gettysburg Address was a mere 272 words in length. How ironic that his speech at one point said,

> The world will little note, nor long remember what we say here.

The world noted and remembered.

Of course, the common problem with younger speakers is not cutting a larger speech down to size like many TED Talk speakers must do. It is about developing enough content to fill the 18 minutes. Ideally, you want your students to be able to give an 18-minute speech, but you cannot start with that length. Just like training for a longer race, you start with short, more seemingly attainable distances at first. This book will show you how to prepare students for a 2-, 5-, 10-, and 15-minute speech so that once they attempt the 18 minutes, it is just a matter of stretching their comfort level a little rather than breaking it.

How you can use TED Talks to teach how to effectively speak in public

Imagine if you wanted to teach someone to be a great basketball player and you were given access to thousands of the best performances by basketball players over the past 30 years. You could watch classics such as Dr. J, Larry Bird, and Kareem

Abdul-Jabbar, contemporaries such as Michael Jordan, Karl Malone, and Charles Barkley, and recent greats LeBron James, Steph Curry, and Giannis Antetokounmpo. Your students would be learning from the best. You could show their styles, their techniques, their strategies, but there are also those players you can show who aren't the superstars but still have something to offer.

This is what it is like using TED Talks to learn to publicly speak. There are over 50,000 TED Talks available on a whole variety of topics. By showing these talks to your students, they will learn what some of the best do in regard to public speaking. Speakers who can teach such skills as:

> Making data interesting: *Hans Rosling "The Best Stats You've Ever Seen"*
>
> Great use of visuals: *David Christian "The History of Our World in 18 minutes"*
>
> Opening with a rhetorical question: *Robin Barrett "Why I Choose to be a Nomad"*
>
> Speaking with passion: *Isabel Allende "How to Live Passionately – No Matter Your Age"*
>
> Use of audience members: *Keith Barry "Brain Magic"*

There will be many more examples of TED Talks that can be used to teach particular public skills spread throughout this book. These can be shown to your students, analyzed, discussed, and ultimately used to improve their speaking abilities.

Because public speaking is so much more than just the words spoken, TED Talks also show students what a good talk looks like. They can watch the speaker as well as listen to them in order to learn the most effective way to reach an audience. They can experience the crowd reactions to see what lands and what doesn't. They can view the visuals to see what other means can be used to communicate. In short, they can see the entire package of public speaking and how someone on the stage can successfully put these elements together in order to command the attention of an audience and communicate with them.

The basic structure of a TED Talk

Essentially, when someone gives a speech, she is telling a story. And all stories have something in common, which is they have a beginning, middle, and an end. Speeches need to have the same structure, although it is labeled as an introduction, the main points, and a conclusion. Although TED Talks have a time limit of about 18 minutes, the same basic structure is used whether the speech is five minutes in length or five hours.

The good news is that your students are already familiar with this structure because it is the same one they use when they are composing a five-paragraph academic essay. It looks like this:

Introduction
    Hook
    Context
    Statement of throughline
    Purpose
    Transition

First main point
    Restatement of throughline
    Evidence to back it up
    Transition

Second main point
    Restatement of throughline
    Evidence to back it up
    Transition

Third main point
    Restatement of throughline
    Evidence to back it up
    Transition

Conclusion
    Restatement of throughline
    Review main points
    Final thought

This is the same format used for a speech. There are differences, of course, between the written word and that which is spoken, but the structure on which all of the information is hung remains the same. This outline can be printed from https://www.thegiftedguy.com/public-speaking. Your students understanding this structure is very important because if the number one goal of a speech is to communicate an idea, then you must use a clear structure that the audience can follow to do so. Without this structure, a speech can feel disjointed and random, causing much confusion, and, more problematic, losing the message.

How developed each of these sections is depends on the time allocated for the speech. If someone is giving a five-minute speech, he cannot afford to take three minutes for his introduction. He simply won't have any time left to deliver his main points. However, if he is giving a 15-minute speech, he should spend a few minutes setting the context and giving folks the background information needed to understand the topic. If he just starts with the main points without an introduction, the audience might not be able to follow. The main points need lots of evidence in a longer speech, but a quick sound bite may be all that can fit into a shorter speech.

The biggest difference between a short and a long speech is the development of the idea. In a shorter speech, space is limited, so the speaker has to be concise and to the point. Just the facts, ma'am. In a longer speech, a speaker can take more time to explain and then crystallize those ideas through the sharing of stories, examples, and evidence to bring them further to life. Of course, the set of challenges that comes with having more time is that there are more chances for the audience to get off track and lose focus as well. The speaker has to make sure everything he is talking about still ties in with the main idea and doesn't shake the audience. This means everything shared has a purpose, and that purpose is more than just taking up space. That purpose is making a case for the idea being shared.

One of the easiest ways for students to relate to the purpose of public speaking is that of a lawyer making a case. When a lawyer speaks in front of the judge, she cannot simply ask for the judge to trust her and believe everything she is saying. She has to convince him and the jury by building a case that makes logical sense and then fortifying it with evidence and research. The stronger the case, the more likely the courtroom will believe her. The lawyer has to lay out her case very clearly, however, and build it up little by little. This is exactly what someone giving a speech must do.

It's more than just the structure though

> **TODD TALK**
>
> To watch a video explaining the basic structure of a speech that can be shown to students, go to:
> https://youtu.be/_TolOxyR72s
>
>

There are other elements that can go into a successful and effective speech. Some of these are:

- Personal story
- Powerful visuals
- Emotional connection
- Vulnerability

All of these, though, are merely techniques and strategies for communicating your main idea. Connecting to the audience is the number one priority. It doesn't matter how you do it but it needs to feel genuine and not part of a show. Chris Anderson, the current curator of TED, talks about what a TED Talk needs in order to be successful:

> **TED TALK**
>
> *TED's Secret to Great Public Speaking by Chris Anderson*
>
> A TED Talk by Chris Anderson, who explains the secret to great public speaking.

He talks about the four things all good TED Talks have in common. They are:

1) Focus on one idea
2) Give audience a reason to care
3) Build the idea piece by piece in audience's language
4) Make the idea worth sharing

Each of these will be talked about in detail throughout the book, but can be defined as the following to your students:

1) Focus on one idea – developing a clear and interesting **throughline**. This is the thesis of the speech, and everything in the speech needs to serve the communication of it.
2) Give audience a reason to care – showing **passion**. It is very difficult for an audience to care if the person speaking does not appear to care. In order to show this, a speaker has to speak with passion. This is more than just words. You have to show it.
3) Build the idea piece by piece in audience's language – **KISS** means to keep it super simple. Just because you are an expert in something doesn't mean your audience is. You have to be able to explain it in steps in such a way that it makes sense to the audience.
4) Make the idea worth sharing – your greatest weapon to gain to attention of your audience is their own **curiosity**. Share something interesting with them that makes them want to know more. Make them think and it will be memorable.

If your students can manage to do these four things, then they will have a worthy speech.

Shining a light

Watching TED Talks is a great way to teach and learn about public speaking. That is why this book will have suggestions for many TED Talks that you can show students to learn specific aspects of public speaking. This also means breaking the speeches down, listening to the audience's reaction, and determining what the speaker did that was effective, and then showing students how to use this for themselves. Here is a checklist that you can use when watching a TED Talk with students to do this very thing:

- How does the speaker begin the speech?
- Does the speaker make you curious to know more?
- Is the speaker's throughline obvious?
- When he/she gets reactions from the audience, what does the speaker do to prompt them?
- What are some ways the speaker connects to the audience?
- Does the speaker maintain your attention and/or focus? If so, what makes you want to continue to listen?
- How would you describe the level of passion the speaker has? Did you think he/she cared about his or her topic?
- How does the speaker use his/her hands while speaking? Does this improve the speech?
- If visuals are used, do these visuals add meaning to your understanding?
- Is there a clear structure with a beginning, middle, and end?
- Does the speech seem long, or does it go by quickly? Why do you think this is?
- Can you tell when the speaker has transitioned to different parts of the speech? If so, what does he/she say to make this clear?
- Does the speaker leave you with something to think about?
- Is it clear the speaker has finished? If so, what does he/she do to make this obvious?

3

Creating a safe space

In order to give students the reassurance that they should not be scared of public speaking, it is imperative that you make your classroom a place where they can take risks and make mistakes and it is OK to do so. This is a safe space from:

- Peers/fellow students
- The teacher
- Themselves

TODD TALK

To watch a video explaining how to create a safe space in your classroom, go to:

https://youtu.be/EMgsfP1dv2c

In order to demonstrate this, I tell students right off the bat that there is no such thing as a perfect speech, that there is always room for improvement. The purpose of scrutinizing a speech is not to find flaws, but instead to learn how we could do things better. An activity that I use to demonstrate this is analyzing one of the most famous speeches of all time: Martin Luther King Jr's *I have a dream* speech https://www.youtube.com/watch?v=vP4iY1TtS3s.

DOI: 10.4324/9781003385981-4

ACTIVITY

Watch MLK's *I have a dream* speech and have a discussion about what he does well and also what could be improved.

You can use a checklist like this to help students with what to look for:

- He speaks with a clear voice that can be understood and heard at all times.
- He uses his hands during the speech to convey emotions.
- He makes eye contact with people in the audience.
- His pace is slow enough to allow the audience to keep up but fast enough to keep them engaged.
- He uses effective hooks (things that get the audience's attention) in his speech.
- He uses pauses or silence in his speech.
- The speech has a clear beginning, middle, and end.
- He ends with something memorable.

These are questions you can use in the discussion:

- What do you think the purpose of the speech was?
- How does he generate emotion other than with his words?
- Do you think the speech is effective in delivering its message, and what makes you believe this?
- What did you think were the most effective aspects of the speech? How were they effective?
- He repeats the line "I have a dream" over and over again. Do you think this was helpful or just annoying?
- What do you think he could have done to make the speech even more impactful?

Ultimately, through their observations, students might find a couple of things that could have been improved.

- Because he was behind a podium, he couldn't use much in the way of body language.
- Some of the audience was behind him, so he was unable to make eye contact as a result.
- He doesn't always speak in the language of the audience (uses big phrases such as "the manacles of segregation and the chains of discrimination" and "this is no time to take the tranquilizing drug of gradualism").
- He is reading his text a lot at the beginning of the speech.

> The purpose of this activity is for students to get the message that there is no such thing as a perfect speech and that mistakes aren't mistakes but rather an opportunity to learn and improve the next time.

This analysis lets students know that we are not looking for gotchas, but rather for help. Speeches can always be made better, which is why feedback should not be punitive, but designed for development.

Creating a culture

You cannot just hope this culture happens by itself. You need to be very deliberate about creating a safe speaking culture in your classroom. There are five suggestions I would give you in order to set up this safe environment. They are:

- Giving students choice
- Helping students find their passion
- Using effective feedback not always tied to a grade
- Creating classroom norms
- Check yourself before you wreck yourself

Giving students choice

Sometimes being a kid sucks. Everyone is telling them what to do. Parents, older siblings, coaches, and other adults tell them what to do rather than them having a say. This happens in school as well. Students are assigned work without any choice in the matter. Because of this, they do not feel as much as part of the learning process. It is difficult to get excited about something that someone else chose for you.

This is why it is important to provide students with as much choice as possible. Sure, there are certain times when choice will not be as much of an option. For example, if you are a science teacher, you would want students to give a speech on something related to that subject area. This doesn't mean, however, that students still couldn't have choice. You could offer a general topic such as space, but then let students choose any aspect of space they find interesting to talk about. It could be Goldilocks planets, the exploration of Mars, or whether the US government should be spending money on sending someone to the moon.

Ideally the only choice you would be making for students would be the purpose of the speech. You might assign them to give an informative or persuasive speech and then let them choose any topic about which they want to inform you or persuade the audience. Even this can be offered as a choice as well.

The main reason for allowing students to make their own choices is so they can find a topic they are excited about. This excitement can carry over into the speech itself. It is much easier to give a speech with passion when you are passionate about what you are speaking about.

Helping students to find their passion

Part of the process of giving a speech for students is finding something they want to talk about. One of the easiest things to talk about is something they care about. The more they care about it, the easier it is to convey passion, which is how to connect with an audience.

Sometimes students need a little help with this. They don't realize what their passions are or what they care about because they have never been given time to think about it. Providing a space for students to have the opportunity to explore their passions will make it easier for them to identify one when tasked with writing a speech.

> **ACTIVITY**
>
> One thing you could do with students to help them find their passion is to take a passion inventory. It might look something like this:

What are your hobbies?

1.
2.
3.
4.
5.

What do you like to do in your free time?

1.

2.

3.

What are the issues on the news or in the world that concern you?

1.

2.

3.

What is your favorite …?

Book:

Movie/TV show:

Sport:

Food:

Videogame:

Music/singer:

You can keep this passion inventory in a file, and whenever students are struggling to identify a topic for their speech, you can look it over with them and use it to make suggestions.

Using effective feedback not always tied to a grade

It is important when you are providing feedback to students on their public speaking skills that it is effective. What is effective feedback, you might ask? Here is an example of ineffective and effective feedback:

1. Your speech was really good.
2. The format used made it easier to follow.

In the first example, the student cannot really pinpoint what made the speech good and so would not know how to repeat this success. The second feedback, however, gave a specific example of what made it good. Now the student can reflect on the format he used and repeat something similar next time.

Here is another example:

1. It was hard to understand you at times.
2. It started at a very quick pace which made it difficult to keep up and understand.

The first piece of feedback is vague. There are a lot of things that can make a speech difficult to understand, such as the pace, volume, fluency, too many ums and ahhs, or using words incorrectly. This feedback is not actionable because the student does not know what caused her to be difficult to understand. The second piece of feedback shows the student the cause of the lack of understanding, so this is something she can work on and prevent in a future speech.

For this pair of examples, try to determine which one is effective and which is not:

1. There were a lot of things you did well, such as speaking loudly, and the visuals you used were very effective.
2. The slides that showed Garbage Island were shocking and grabbed my attention.

You might think it is the first one. After all, it is longer and it points out two things, but it is actually the second one. The first one does not provide enough specific detail for the student to see what was done well. It mentions speaking loudly. Speaking loudly is not what we want students to do; we don't want them to be obnoxious. We want them to speak loud enough. It needs to be an appropriate volume. When focusing on the visuals being effective, were certain ones better than others? What about those were effective? This is what the second comment does. It lets the student know which photo was the one that really stood out so the next time she might find a visual like this if she wants a similar effect.

As a final test, what pattern do you notice about the three ineffective and effective feedback examples provided so far ...

Give up ...?

All of the ineffective examples use the pronoun "you". Because of this, the feedback is directed at the students themselves, not the skill they are trying to display. This may cause students to think they are being attacked or criticized. The effective examples, on the other hand, point specifically to the skill that was done well or needed to be improved. This puts students in the mindset of the skill needing to be fixed rather than themselves. It keeps it from being personal.

Effective feedback typically has these qualities, which will be discussed in more detail in the chapter on finding your voice:

- Is specific/focused
- Is actionable
- Is about the skill, not the student
- Is designed to improve, not to criticize
- Is written or spoken in a student-friendly manner that can be understood
- Is timely

Feedback can have a large effect on student learning. Marzano (2001) found an effect size for feedback of 0.76, which translates roughly into a 28 percentile point difference in average achievement. Hattie (2009) found a similar effect size of 0.73 for feedback. However, feedback and a grade are two different things. Black and William (2009) found that 60% of students made significantly greater improvements when feedback was not tied to a grade. Sometimes, because of our thinking that everything has to have a grade in order to be measured, we grade things we don't really need to. And whether we mean to or not, by giving a student a

B or C, we are essentially telling them that they did something wrong; otherwise, they would have received an A. Of course, the opposite end of that argument is that we give too many As, and this grade inflation causes students to think there is no room for improvement. It is better to evaluate using a measurement that does not equate to a percentage point or a letter grade.

Creating classroom norms

It is all well and good for you, the teacher, to offer a safe space, but you are leaving stones unturned if you do not work with your entire class to help them find ways to provide effective feedback in a manner that is helpful to the classroom culture. This way, students are not reliant on one voice to provide ways to improve and instead can develop their speeches from suggestions given by their fellow students.

How the class can create such a culture is by using norms. Norms are not rules; they do not have punishments attached to them. They are simply expectations. And they are not the expectations of the teacher. They are the expectations of everyone in the class as to how things should be. Because of this, norms should be created by the class rather than handed down by the teacher.

> **ACTIVITY**
>
> As a class you should determine what the expectations are in order to create a safe space. You can use this protocol to create them:
>
> Materials:
>
> - sticky notes
> - chart paper/whiteboard
> - writing utensils
>
> *Step 1*: Give each student half a dozen or so sticky notes and a writing utensil. Instruct the following: "What do you need in order to feel safe to speak in front of the class?"
>
> *Step 2*: Allow people 5–10 minutes to write down ideas. Make sure they know to put one idea per post-it note.

Step 3: Once it appears everyone has finished, invite them to come up to the whiteboard/chart paper and cluster similar ideas together.

Step 4: As the facilitator, come to the board and read the ideas.

Step 5: As each idea is shared, the facilitator leads a group discussion, making sure everyone agrees to the idea or gathers more information why the person who suggested it did so. If everyone agrees it is a valid idea, it is crafted into a concise norm.

Step 6: The facilitator should write down, either on a whiteboard or on a piece of chart paper, the norms that the group has come up with.

Step 7: The facilitator will eventually need to type up the norms and provide copies for everyone.

A few norms that might come up:

- When you give feedback, make sure it is helpful.
- The audience should be paying attention.
- No laughing at people or making fun of them.
- Applaud whenever someone finishes.
- Need time to settle down right before speaking.

By creating these norms, the culture of the classroom has been set by including student voices as well. The buy-in for this has a much better chance of happening because students had a say. Then they will be more willing to provide feedback of their own because that is the expectation they set.

Check yourself before you wreck yourself

One of the most powerful voices in the classroom is your own. Sometimes as teachers we forget the impact our words have, even when we are not intending for them to carry as much weight as they do. Because of this, you need to choose your words carefully.

Of course, remember every time you are pointing your finger at someone, there are three fingers pointing back at you. I say this because I tend to be a sarcastic person. I had a student once who came up to me, proud as can be, and showed me his test.

"Mr. Stanley, Mr. Stanley. I did much better on this test than I did on the last one".

The smartass in me couldn't resist the urge to say, "Well, it couldn't have been much worse".

I came to find out later from the math teacher that she overheard this student complaining about my comment by his locker and added how he felt he couldn't do anything well. Of course, this was not my intention, but that did not matter.

We want to make sure that when we are providing feedback, it is effective. It doesn't mean it always has to be good news, and you certainly shouldn't sugarcoat it, but it does need to be devoid of maliciousness. You need to keep in mind your bedside manner and have the mindset of always encouraging a way to make things better.

Shining a spotlight

Here is a TED Talk you might want to watch with students before trying to establish a safe classroom:

Some possible discussion questions:

TED TALK

Why We Fear Public Speaking by Taylor Williams is a TED Talk that explains how to redefine how we look at public speaking. Students can watch it on their own or as a class to discuss.

- Why do you suppose people feel vulnerable when public speaking?
- Do you feel vulnerable? If so, how so?
- How would you define public speaking?
- What do you think she means by presenting our "authentic self"?
- What do you think imagining people in their underwear has to do with vulnerability?
- Do you feel like you are being judged when speaking in public?
- Do you agree with the statement that 93% of what we communicate comes through our body language?

- If you do, what is going to be important when giving your presentation?
- Which advice do you think was the most helpful for you, and why?
- What are ways that you speak publicly in your everyday life?
- What do you think about the statement "public speaking is not perfection"?

4

How to get started – the two-minute bio speech

When you are introducing public speaking to your class, there will be many people who feel as though they do not have anything to say. Of course, everyone has something to say, but convincing them of this can be a challenge. That is why for their first speech you give them a topic they do know a lot about: themselves.

I always begin public speaking in my class by having students give a two-minute talk about themselves. I do this for three reasons:

1. This is a topic that requires no research and they already know a lot about it
2. It helps them learn a little bit about themselves and how they see themselves
3. The rest of the class and I get to learn more about the student

Before they begin to develop their speech, I spend a lot of time talking about the importance of a throughline.

The importance of a throughline

We all know what a thesis is, right? A thesis is the main idea of an essay that drives the writing. Everything in the essay is in service to the thesis, which the author is trying to convince the reader of by using examples, details, and research. It acts as the North Star the reader is following and it focuses the writing.

In public speaking, this is known as the throughline. This is actually a better term for it anyway because it is literally the line that runs through the entire piece. Everything is connected to this line, and any time someone gets off it, that is when clarity is sacrificed. The best speeches have a clear throughline that is obvious to the audience. If you listen to a speech and are not sure what the throughline is, then the speaker has strayed too far from it.

Examples of throughlines you might commonly hear:

- Why you should vote for me (political)
- The lesson to be learned here is … (moral)
- How you can solve this problem (lesson)
- This is what this book is about … (informative)
- Why should you buy this product (advertisement)
- The advice I can give you on doing this is … (experiential)
- Is this movie any good (review)
- This is better than that because … (argumentative)
- We are here to honor the graduates today (commencement)
- I have a great idea (pitch)

The throughline defines the purpose of the speech. It gives those who are listening direction. It tells them what they should be listening for. You would think this would be obvious in many cases. Most times, people know why they are at a particular speech. They may be attending a conference, sitting in a meeting, or participating in a special occasion such as a graduation. But remember this valuable piece of advice: ALWAYS ASSUME THE AUDIENCE IS IGNORANT.

Even though they are in a banquet hall sitting next to people in nice clothing, being served food with a woman in a wedding gown and men in tuxedos at the front of the room, reminding them they are at a wedding and what you are there to celebrate is never a bad idea. Even though they chose to attend your session based on a title and a written blurb about what the speech is going to be covering, tell them why they are here today and what you hope to accomplish. Even though they are sitting in Mr. Clarkson's fourth-period social studies class and everyone in the room has been assigned the speech of why the Enlightenment Period was so important, present it to them as though they haven't been studying it along with you.

The throughline not only keeps the audience focused, it keeps the speaker focused as well. If the speaker sticks to the throughline and everything talked about ties into this, then the message will be clear. It is when the speaker deviates from the throughline that the message becomes muddled.

Figure 4.1 is an example of what a throughline would look like in a speech about the benefits of going for a walk.

You'll notice that everything used in the talk, the story, the anecdote, the statistics, the research, and the visuals, all connect to the throughline. It is the evidence that is used to make the throughline's point. It propels the throughline forward and strengthens it with each new piece of evidence. It makes the case for walking.

And yet sometimes in an effort to find content, people get side-tracked. This comes off as rambling, which causes the speech to lack focus. So guess what the audience is going to do? That's right, they are going to lose focus because there is nothing to keep them on track. A speech that loses its throughline might look like Figure 4.2.

Some of the parts about Roosevelt answer the throughline of why he was one of the best presidents, such as the anecdotes and statistics about what he did while he was president. However, the background information about his early life does not, nor does the photo of him when he was in the Rough Riders, before he was president. Although the anecdote about how people confused Theodore and Franklin Roosevelt might get some laughs, it doesn't say anything about his presidency. In fact, there is no section determining the criteria of what makes him one of the best presidents, nor does it compare him to any others. The quote at the end could be used for the throughline as long as the speaker makes a connection between the quote and how Theodore Roosevelt used it to identify his foreign policy position. But it

42 ◆ Letting Student Voices Shine

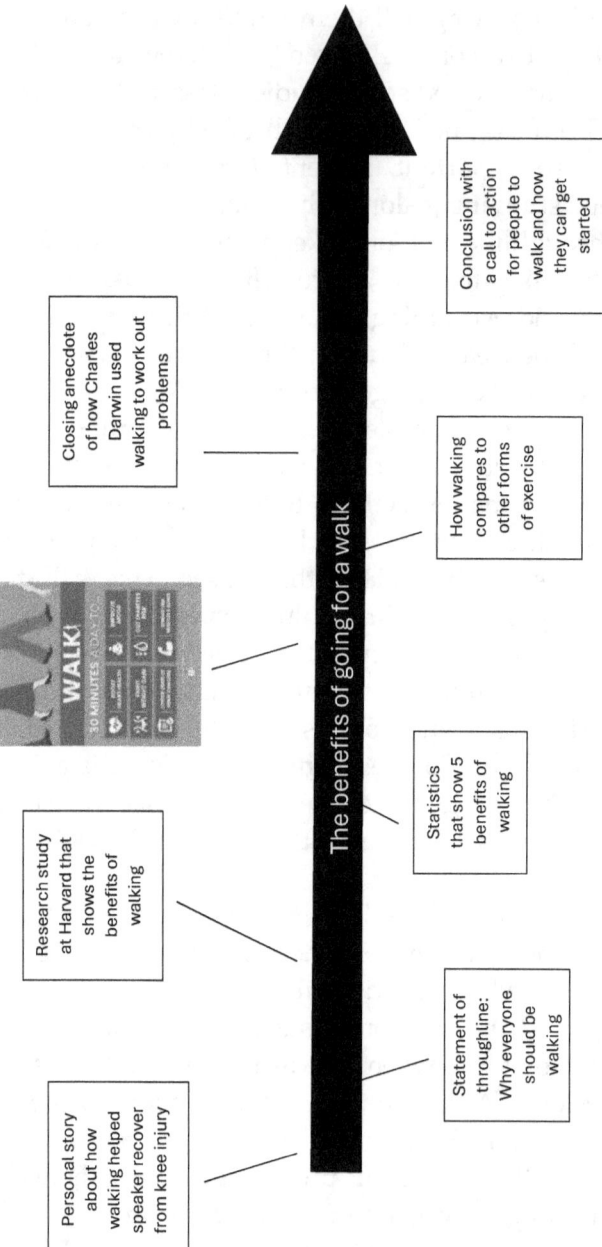

FIGURE 4.1

Getting started – two-minute bio speech ◆ 43

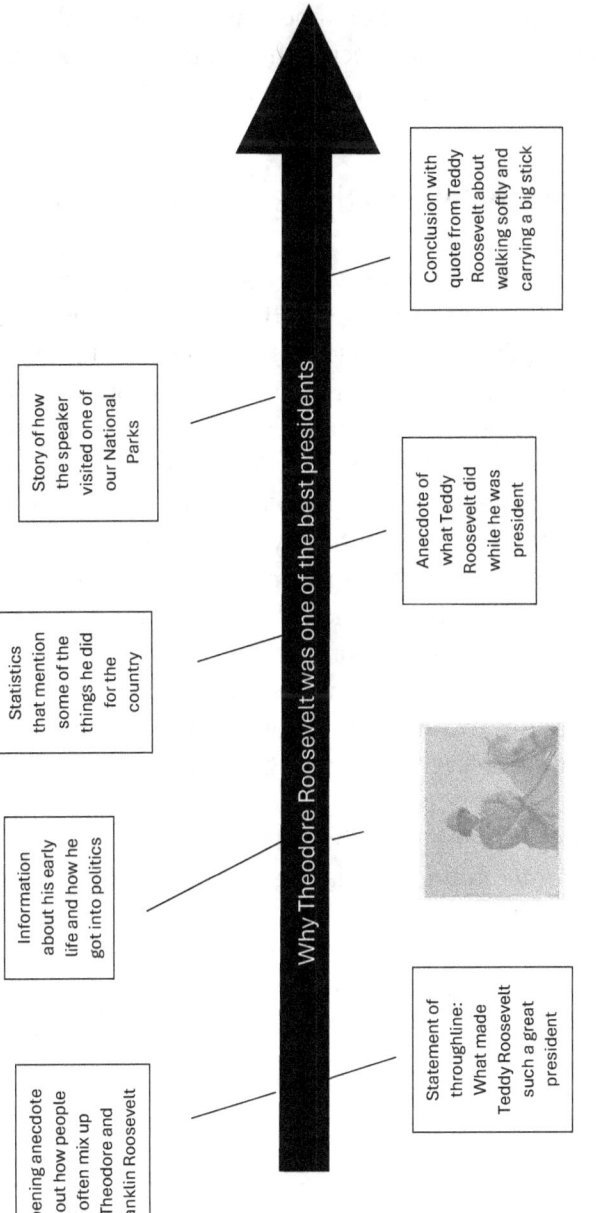

FIGURE 4.2

was given when he was governor of New York, not president, so the connection to his presidency must be clear.

While everything spoken about was connected to the topic, it did not connect to the specific throughline. There is a very big difference between the throughline and the topic.

The difference between a throughline and a topic

The topic of a speech is *what* you are going to be talking about. The throughline of the speech is the *specific idea* about the topic that you are going to be sharing. For example, the topic of your speech is tennis. But there are a lot of things you can share about tennis. It could be how the game works. It could be the history of tennis. It could be showing how to do a specific skill in tennis.

Where speakers get into trouble and thus cause confusion is when they stay on topic but stray from the specific idea being shared about the topic. For example, the throughline is how to play tennis, and yet the speaker talks about their favorite tennis player without any connection to this.

The throughline might change based on the purpose of the speech. Here are examples of throughlines all about tennis, but the throughline changes depending on the purpose of the speech:

- Expository/Informative – The rules of tennis
- Argumentative/Persuasive – Tennis is much better than pickleball
- Demonstrative – How do you hit a backhand in tennis?
- Oratorical – Why tennis is a lifelong sport
- Motivational – You should be playing tennis for your health

Tennis is still mentioned in every throughline, but the lens through which you are looking at it focuses on a different thing. It is important as the speaker that you focus on the throughline and not just the topic.

Here is a TED Talk that you can use with your students to make sure they understand the difference between a topic and a throughline:

This is a talk seemingly about her time spent as an exchange student in Peru, but that is the topic. The throughline is about taking chances. The title of the talk is *A Leap of Faith*, words she never speaks during the speech but shows through every story she tells. Stories such as:

- Going to Camp Mary Orton with a couple she barely knows and meeting new people with different accents

> **TED TALK LESSON**
>
> *A Leap of Faith by Caroline Shapiro* at TEDxYouth@Columbus in 2013 is a TEDx talk that does an excellent job of establishing her throughline through a series of personal narratives.

- Traveling to Peru as an exchange student in a country where not many speak her language
- Jumping into the Amazon River at the end of her trip with all of its dangers such as piranhas
- Giving the TED Talk itself in front of an audience

She finishes the talk by restating her throughline in different words: "unless it's immoral or illegal, always say yes". In other words, take a chance. She sticks to this throughline with everything she talks about in the speech. Even the hook story at the beginning, where she faints at her Peruvian high school, gives the message of taking a chance.

This is a good TED Talk to show to students and have them guess what the throughline is. Most will say being an exchange student which is the topic. Help them to see the throughline and not the topic.

Writing a solid throughline

Here is the thing about a speech: it is not intended to be a mystery. People should not be guessing the message of your speech. This is not a fairy tale such as *The Three Little Pigs*, which seemingly is a story about pigs getting stalked by a wolf but really is a lesson about how when you cut corners and take the easy path, there are consequences to pay. The lesson in that story is not clearly stated but must be implied by the audience. For a speech, it should be very obvious to your audience what it is you are here to tell them. There should be no implying. This all starts with a clear throughline where you lay out what it is you want them to get from your speech.

You want to control the message by giving it to them so that nothing is lost in translation. This message should be stated in your throughline, which should also be repeated throughout. You can even display this throughline on a slide if you are presenting a slidedeck.

It all begins with a well-written throughline. It is the foundation on which you set everything else atop. A weak throughline and the speech will fall apart. A strong throughline and it can carry you through even the most difficult crowds.

How a throughline is written is by dividing the topic by its specific focus and adding the purpose of the speech. The formula looks something like this:

$$(\text{topic} \div \text{focus}) + \text{purpose} = \text{throughline}$$

So if someone was wanting to do a speech about dogs, she would need to figure out what exactly about dogs she was going to focus on. After all, she can't just randomly discuss dogs. There needs to be an area of focus to make a central point. Their worth as a pet could be one approach because she likes dogs and has one of her own that she can draw on experiences about.

$$(\text{topic} \div \text{focus}) \quad \text{worth as a pet}$$

The purpose is what the speaker is trying to do for an audience. Is the purpose to inform, convince them of something, or inspire them? The purpose of this particular dog speech is argumentative. This means the speaker needs to make an argument out of the main idea. There are lots of different arguments that could be made, such as that dogs are the smartest animal, they are the most helpful, they are great with kids, and they can cause you to be more active and thus healthy.

As you work through this with your students, they can choose whichever one they want, but let's say for the sake of argument that the speaker decides to make the argument that dogs are the best pet.

(worth as a pet) + argument = dogs are best because of affection

The specific argument in this case is that dogs are best because they are such loving animals. This is the "why" of the argument. When this is all put together, you have the following throughline:

Dogs are the best pets because they show such loving affection

Just like a math problem, you can show students how to run it backward to check that everything is included.

Dogs are the best pets because they show such loving affection

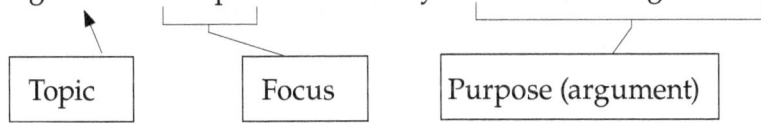

| Topic | Focus | Purpose (argument) |

That makes this a solid throughline.

TODD TALK

To watch a video explaining this throughline formula to students, go to:
https://youtu.be/ NlyatKcGMm0

Finding their throughline

Now that students know what a throughline is, this brings us back to their bio speech. This is good practice as to whether they know the difference between a topic and a throughline. If they just talk about themselves, the topic, they typically will be very random and will list off a lot of different things about themselves that have no cohesive whole. You want them to tell a single story about themselves, a main idea or theme, that gets to the heart of who they are.

I will give students the guiding question for their throughline, which is "What makes you who you are?" There are all sorts of possibilities. Here are some examples of throughlines that students have come up with over the years:

- Your likes/dislikes
- Something you think everyone should know about you
- Your favorites (i.e., movie, book, music, hobbies, food)
- How your friends and family would describe you
- Who are your idols or the people you look up to and why?
- What would you like to do when you grow up?
- Where have you traveled, or would you like to travel?

Engineering design process for pre-planning

Then I give students time to prepare their speech using the engineering design process which looks like Figure 4.3.

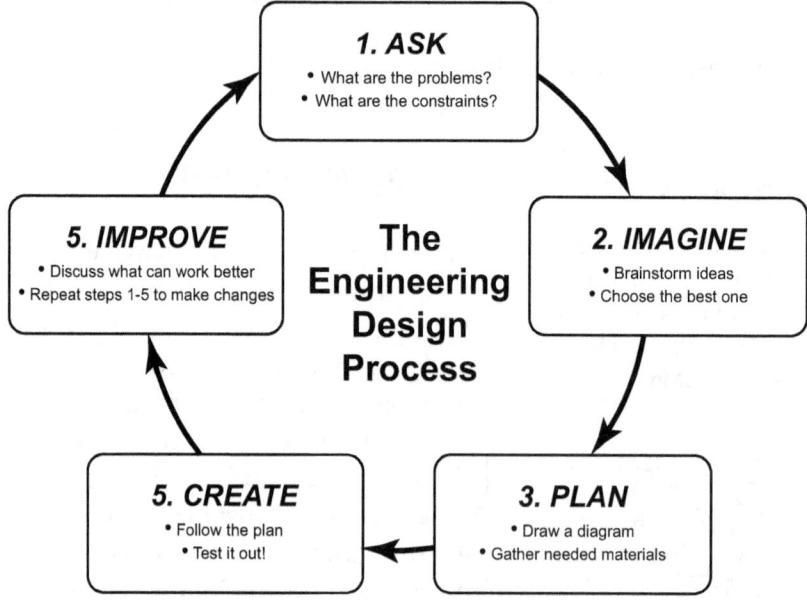

FIGURE 4.3

These are the steps most engineers use when trying to solve a problem. It is also is a great way to plan the writing of a speech.

Step #1 of the task has already been done. Students have considered their throughline, which answers the problem of who they are. Step #2 involves them imagining, which involves thinking of all of the anecdotes, examples, and details that illustrate the throughline. Typically, an academic essay or a speech has three supporting points. Encourage them to come up with more than this in this brainstorming session so that they have some to choose from. Suggest that they come up with at least six. In the planning, which is step #3, they will narrow down these ideas to the best possible three. "Best" can have a whole lot of different meanings. It might mean the examples that seem the most interesting. It could be the ones that will make people laugh the most if that is the tone the student wants to set for the speech. Maybe it is the ones that provide the most detail. Whatever criteria they choose, it should be the ones that best bring their throughline to life.

Now that they have done all of this pre-planning, they can begin to create the speech, step #4. Here, students are fleshing out the ideas, recalling the details of the examples they wish to use, and building the content which will make up their speech. Since this is only a two-minute speech, they don't have a whole lot of time to get too detailed, but there does need to be enough for the audience to see what the speaker is talking about.

The final step is improving, where most speeches are made or broken. Because a speech is given in a public speaking forum, the only way to know whether it works or not is to say it out loud. This rehearsal process lets the speaker know whether something sounds as good as he thought it did, whether there are any awkward phrases, and to see how much time it actually will take. If one practices the speech and it is only a minute and a half, he can add more details in order to ensure time management. If it is three minutes, he knows he will need to cut something or explain something with more conciseness. Step #5 is the most important part of the shaping of a speech. It indicates whether it works or not. And if it doesn't, changes need to be made to improve it.

Students should think of it as a piece of pottery that needs to be shaped and smoothed in certain places.

I typically give students 30 minutes to prepare for their bio speech. I break it down within the engineering design process like this:

1. Ask – five minutes
2. Imagine – five minutes
3. Plan – five minutes
4. Create – eight minutes
5. Improve – seven minutes

I let students know when they should move on to the next step of the engineering design process. This helps students with their time management.

By using the engineering design process as a structure, students have a better chance of creating something that has focus because it has been well thought out and put together in an orderly fashion rather than just throwing things together.

Tips for their first speech

> **TODD TALK**
>
> To watch a video of my bio and throughline as an example of a bio speech to show to students, watch here:
>   https://youtu.be/drObmH6Cbrs
>
>

Once they are ready to give their speech, I provide some tips that they should remember. These include:

- Speak slowly and clearly
- Have good posture when speaking
- Put your hands either to the side or in front of you
- Try to avoid *umms* and *buts*
- If you get side-tracked, don't panic
- Look out at your audience
- Finish strong
- Most importantly, have fun

Feedback for the first speech

For this particular speech, I offer little to no feedback. The reason is that I just want them to give their first speech to see how it feels. This is not about quality; it is about completing the act. Getting the monkey off their back, so to speak.

Make sure you congratulate students on giving their first speech. Also, remind them that nobody died. Sure, it may have been tough to get that first speech out, but now that they have done it, what is to stop them from giving their next speech? I usually just clap, encourage the rest of the class to do the same according to our norms, and acknowledge the student for getting through it. I do tell them how long their speech was, but not as a criticism, merely as information so they know how they managed their time and what the length feels like.

Reflection after the speech

Although I do not provide effective feedback after this first speech, I do want students to consider for themselves what worked and what needed work. It is important for students to be self-reflective if they are going to be able to improve their public speaking skills. This means understanding why. If they think they did not do a very good job, what is the evidence to back this assertion? If they feel as though they were successful with something, what led them to believe this?

Reflection is about finding tangible examples that can be acted upon, either by continuing to do it if it led to success, or figuring out something else if it did not go as hoped. I have them ponder the following questions to provide guidance:

- How did you feel about your speech?
- Did you communicate what you wanted to?
- What do you think you did well?
- Where is there room for improvement?

Students do not necessarily need to write these thoughts out, but you do want to get them in the habit of thinking about them and processing after they have given a speech. This is how someone gets better as a public speaker. This acts as guidance for how to do this and the questions they should be asking themselves.

If time allows, I ask students to give the reflection as a mini-speech to a partner or small group, where they verbally share their conclusions from their speech. I like to use mini-speeches as a safe place to speak in public without being judged. What I ask of students is that they focus on something they want to work on while giving the speech, but other than that, I don't care how good the reflection is. So if in their bio speech, they reflect that they didn't show much emotion, this is something they can work on in the mini-speech.

Shining a light

We want students to work their way into the waters of public speaking by dipping a toe rather than just being thrown into the deep end. It is very important to have a life preserver should things not go well, and the throughline acts as this. A strong throughline allows the speaker to pull themselves in, even in the most treacherous of waters. That is why teaching it clearly and being sure they understand it is so important. If they can see this and stay focused on it, then the audience stands a better chance of understanding what is being talked about.

The thing to remember about writing, public speaking, or any other such form is that its sole purpose is to communicate. If you are not doing that clearly, if you lose sight of the throughline and lose your audience as a result, your message will not be understood.

> **TED TALK**
>
> Here is a TED Talk that explains the importance of the throughline: *The Through Line by Chad Willett.*

5

Finding your voice

This book is all about giving your students the confidence to use their voice. We want to hear what our students have to say, and we want to teach them how to make their voice heard even beyond their school years and into their professional and personal lives. This is why their actual voice is the major focus for their first speech.

The problem with many novice speakers is that because they lack the confidence to speak, this shows in the way they deliver their words. I have heard many first speeches given with the liveliness of a wet blanket. What causes students to sound so boring? Oftentimes they rely on their written speech and thus end up sounding like the navigation voice on your maps app. So how do you prevent a speaker from sounding like a robot?

The main culprit is the monotone delivery. When a voice is monotone, it is very steady and does not fluctuate in any way. This is what it sounds like when you are reading something out loud, especially something you are unfamiliar with.

In public speaking, we are presenting. In order to prevent sounding like a robot, we need to make our students aware of the difference between reading and presenting.

> **TODD TALK**
>
> Here is a video demonstrating the difference between reading and presenting that can be shown to students:
> https://youtu.be/65o4-laPP78
>
>

> **TED TALKS**
>
> Here are two TED Talks, one presented and one read. See if your students can tell the difference rather than telling them which one.
> Talk 1: *Flow, the Secret to Happiness by Mihaly Csikszentmihalyi*
> Talk 2: *Your Elusive Creative Genius by Elizabeth Gilbert*

The difference between reading and presenting

One way to determine the difference is to see it in action. There are many good TED Talks out there, and nearly all of them are well-written. But not all of them are well-spoken. I often have students watch the first five minutes of these two TED Talks. Then we talk about the differences between them and what makes them so different.

After watching these, hopefully, students will plainly see that Talk 2 is so much more engaging and upbeat. Talk 1, on the other hand, seems flat and droll. This is so ironic because Csikszentmihalyi's topic is "flow, the secret to happiness", which is a very positive topic. Gilbert's, on the other hand, is about the immense expectations people have about her follow-up book and how depressing this is.

You will want to make sure students either notice or you point out why one of these talks is so much more engaging. Some of the reasons they might focus on are:

- He speaks in monotone; she speaks with enthusiasm
- She uses her hands a lot, while he crosses his arms or puts them behind his back. At one point, he even blocks his mouth while stroking his beard
- He stands in one place most of the time; she moves around the stage
- She explains the why, it is difficult to figure out his why

- He speaks to the audience as if it is a lecture; she speaks as though it is a conversation

How do we get students to deliver their speeches without them sounding so blah? We let them practice reading with life.

Letting them practice bringing words to life

In order to get students used to presenting rather than reading, I typically give students a monologue to read aloud. The sole purpose of having them do this is to try to instill some emotion into the words on the page. I direct them to a site, https://www.dramanotebook.com/monologues-kids-teenagers/, with tons of monologues and let them pick one. They are then are tasked with giving the monologue aloud to a partner or small group, making sure they present it in a conversational tone rather than read it in a wooden manner.

Here is an example monologue from Tom Sawyer:

Well, if that ain't just like you, Huck Finn. You CAN get up the infant-schooliest ways of going at a thing. Why, hain't you ever read any books at all? – Baron Trenck, nor Casanova, nor Benvenuto Chelleeny, nor Henri IV, nor none of them heroes? Who ever heard of getting a prisoner loose in such an old-maidy way as that? No; the way all the best authorities does is to saw the bed-leg in two, and leave it just so, and swallow the sawdust, so it can't be found, and put some dirt and grease around the sawed place so the very keenest seneskal can't see no sign of it's being sawed, and thinks the bed-leg is perfectly sound. Then, the night you're ready, fetch the leg a kick, down she goes; slip off your chain, and there you are. Nothing to do but hitch your rope ladder to the battlements, shin down it, break your leg in the moat – because a rope ladder is nineteen foot too short, you know – and there's your horses and your trusty vassles, and they scoop you up and fling you across a saddle, and away you go to your native Langudoc, or Navarre, or wherever it is. It's gaudy, Huck. I wish there was a moat to this cabin. If we get time, the night of the escape, we'll dig one.

> **TODD TALK**
>
> To watch a video of Verlin providing some strategies for not sounding like a robot that can be shown to students go to:
>
> https://www.youtube.com/watch?v=nQZWGZMLD9g
>
>

This is not an acting class by any means, but it is trying to get speakers to understand the difference between reading and presenting. One analogy I give to put students in the correct mindset is to imagine they are speaking to a friend rather than an audience of people. What would their tone be? Would they be so formal with this friend? Wouldn't their demeanor be more relaxed? That is the way a speech should be approached.

Avoid fillers

One of the common things speakers do when giving a speech is say lots of *ums* and *uhs*. In fact, these are so prevalent in our speech that many podcasts actually edit these out so that it seems as though people are talking without them when that is not the case. There are other common fillers that we use, usually when we aren't exactly sure what we are going to say next. Some of these are:

- Like
- So
- Okay
- You know
- Well
- Actually
- I guess
- Er
- Hmm
- Really

In conversation, these fillers are perfectly acceptable. In a formal speech, however, they are discouraged. Saying a few of these words in your speech is not a problem. It only becomes an issue when you say them too often to the point where they become a distraction. The occasional *um* or *like* is not going to wreck your speech. Saying *like* 47 times in a five-minute speech, as I had one student do, completely takes the listener away from the content of what is being said. But it doesn't even have to be this extreme. The use of umm just a few times in a row can become very noticeable.

> **TED-ED TALK**
>
> A TED-Ed on why we use fillers such as *like* or *um*:
>   *Why Do We, Like, Hesitate When We, Um, Speak?* By Lorenzo García-Amaya
>   And here is a video on strategies for not doing this: *How to Stop Saying "Um", "Like", and "You Know"* by The Distilled Man https://www.youtube.com/watch?v=W995352_kkw

It is important for students to identify their particular filler word. Awareness is important if you are going to stop using it so much. For instance, my filler word is the word *so*. When I am drawing a conclusion or starting a new idea, I often say this word. I did not even realize this until I began making YouTube videos about teaching and watched the playback. I couldn't believe how many times I said "so" in my first few videos. Once I realized my overuse of the word, I was able to cut it down enough that it was not completely removed, but it was certainly less repetitive and noticeable.

Have students partner up with someone and just have a natural conversation, something like what they did last weekend or what their favorite movie is. It is likely their filler word will reveal itself. Have the other person listen for it and identify it. Once a student is aware of it, they can watch out for it in their speeches.

What does practice look like

One of my favorite quotes is by Arthur Ashe, the tennis player. He won three Grand Slam tournaments, the biggest tournaments in the world. He said of preparation, "One important key to success is self-confidence. An important key to self-confidence is preparation".

If students want to build confidence as a speaker, they *will* need to practice. This preparation does five things:

1. Makes them familiar with the pronunciation of words so that they do not fumble with them
2. Allows them to find mistakes or things that are not working and change them
3. Gives them an idea of how much time it takes and then adjusting to add or subtract content to fit this allotment
4. Allows them to practice non-speaking communication such as eye contact, posture, hand movements, and other non-verbals
5. Gets them comfortable with the flow of the speech so that it becomes more natural and gives them more confidence in giving it

Now, just because someone practices does not guarantee that the speech is going to be great. Students need to practice with purpose. For example, if you want to become a better golfer, you don't just play a bunch of golf. You focus on something, say your short game, and then you work on that, pinpointing strategies to make it better.

Say in a student's previous speech she had a habit of not looking at the audience. She should practice this by looking at specific things in the room she is practicing in. She needs to try to make her practice as much like the real thing as possible. If a student is going to be standing while giving the speech, she should practice giving it while standing. If the assignment is to have a slide deck while presenting, she should practice speaking while advancing the slides.

Practice should not simply involve reading through the speech. There are many other things that go into its presentation, those things should be practiced as well. It helps to have students record their speeches and watch them. They will see and hear many things they didn't notice before.

When I first began as a teacher, I needed to videotape some lessons. I noticed when watching the videos that I taught to one side of the classroom. Instead of looking all around the room, my focus and attention leaned toward the right side of the room, leaving the left side unattended. I had never realized this before, and no one had ever said anything. After seeing this, I became more conscious about presenting to the entire room and saw in later videos that I had made the correction. We don't know what we don't know. Seeing is believing sometimes.

There is no magic number, but I would advise students to at least practice a speech three times, with a different purpose each time. You could advise them:

- First time – just get the words out and make sure it all makes sense. Note places where you seem to stumble and adjust to those.
- Second time – time the speech to make sure it is the length you want it to be.

(Not all speeches have a limit, but I try to get my students into the habit of giving a speech of a specific length so that they can better manage their time.)

- Third time – make sure everything goes together. If you have a slidedeck, does the speaking match up with it? Does your non-verbal communication match your enthusiasm for the speech? Does the tone of your voice match the tone of your topic?

Students should think of the speech as the draft of an essay and the practice they are doing as revisions of that draft. Each time, the purpose is to make it a little better and to fix issues. If students give their speech the same way all three times without any adjustments, they are not going to improve the speech at all. They are simply giving the same version with flaws three times.

I always tell students to have their rubric out when they practice to make sure they are addressing all of the elements that will be looked for. I sometimes give them a checklist to use to help with this:

Checklist for the TED-Ed Speech

_____ What is being talked about connects to your throughline.
_____ The throughline is clearly stated throughout the entire speech
_____ Speech has a clear beginning, middle, and end that are divided appropriately among the time.
_____ The speech should be between 4:30–5:30 minutes in length.

Voice

_____ Speaks fluently, avoiding too many *ums* and *likes*.
_____ The pace is appropriate to what is being talked about but always allows the audience to understand the speaker clearly.
_____ Presents rather than reads and doesn't sound monotone.

Slide Deck

_____ Has just one idea per slide.
_____ There are more than five visuals used in the presentation.
_____ The visuals add to the content of the speech by providing additional information or demonstrating a point the speaker is making.

This and the checklists in this book can be printed off my website at https://www.thegiftedguy.com/public-speaking

To memorize or not to memorize

One solution to not sounding like a robot is to avoid reading. Unfortunately, when you have to speak anywhere from 1,000 to sometimes 3,000 words, it is hard to remember that many words. I have had students who were able to do it. They memorized their speeches and gave them without notes. I have also had some attempt this, and because they had memorized blocks of text triggered by spoken lines, if they forgot the spoken line, they couldn't access the entire block of content. They actually froze in the middle of their speech and had trouble getting themselves back on track.

Then there are those who have their speech on index cards or a document (remind students not to not read it off their cell phone; it looks really bad). Having this in front of the speaker is good for making sure they stay focused and don't forget anything. Unfortunately, it can also look unprofessional. There are very few TED speakers who you see holding notes. And when they do, it doesn't always look the best.

When you use notes, you have to hold them, which takes away one or both of your hands that could be able to use for non-verbals. In the aforementioned speech, the speaker tries in vain to use the one hand he has free as much as he would use two. But that in itself is not the issue. The issue is that the cards become a crutch, and he ends up reading them too often. The first words he speaks are "I love infographics", but it is delivered with the enthusiasm of an action star from the 1980s. I just don't believe that he loves infographics. About two minutes into the speech, he looks down at one of his cards, pauses for an awkward moment, and says without any feeling, "I get excited when I get lots of data to play with".

> **TED TALK**
>
> *The Simple Genius of a Good Graphic by Tommy McCall*
>
> This speaker not only uses notecards, but it ends up making the speech very wooden.

As an audience member, I don't buy this excitement because it is delivered with zero excitement. Anytime he is on screen, he is looking down at his cards, taking away the valuable eye contact that helps with connection. About 5:15 minutes into the speech, he breaks a sentence up in an unnatural manner. He says, "Graphics that help us think faster or see a book's worth of information on a single page are the key to unlocking … new discoveries". Because he looks down for a moment to find the words, he breaks up the reveal of his statement, taking its effectiveness away.

It is a shame too because the speech itself is well structured and has a lot of great information, especially its visuals. But the way he presents it does not connect to the audience. The note cards are actually acting as a barrier between him and his audience.

The answer that I have found that works best is sort of a combination. It involves rehearsing your speech enough times that you are familiar with it, although not every word is memorized, and then using the slidedeck to act as an outline to know what to speak about next. The question, of course, is what if you do not use a slide deck. I would say over half of actual TED Talks use slidedecks. I personally prefer to use slidedecks because audience members usually fall into one of two categories: those who are auditory learners and those who are visual learners. Speech givers also fall into those two categories as well. Because of this, some students can memorize their speech without any issue because they are auditory learners who, while hearing it over and over through their practice, are able put it into their working memory. The visual learner, on the other hand, might find this task a bit more challenging. By including a slidedeck or visuals, they not only help the audience to get a clearer picture of what they are talking about in their speech, but they also give themselves a better idea of what they are supposed to be talking about because the visuals remind them of the details that they might have otherwise forgotten or overlooked.

This is really about personal preference. Just as there is no one way to do most things, students need to find what works best for them and use that. This might take some trial and error. Just make sure students know what their options are and have good reasons for choosing them.

Dealing with stage fright

The most difficult thing for students to learn in public speaking is not the structure, the body language, nor the incorporation of visuals. The most difficult thing to overcome is stage fright. The reason is that no one ever actually overcomes stage fright. It is an inevitable by-product of giving a speech to others.

This TED-Ed Talk points out three very important lessons in addition to its other advice. The first is perspective. The main cause of stage fright is that, in public speaking, the person is in front of others. Put yourself in the shoes of your students. School is difficult enough as it is. And when they are in front of others, they are being judged. The judgment might be positive or it might be

> **TED-ED TALK**
>
> *The Science of Stage Fright (and How to Overcome It)* by Mikael Cho is a TED-Ed talk about the science behind stage fright and some strategies for adapting to it.

critical; it might be warranted or it may not. Regardless, it is in the crowd's nature to judge those who are in a public forum. There is no preventing this judgment from others, even in the friendliest of crowds, but it causes a lot of stress and anxiety for some. We have all been exposed to social media enough to know that there are a lot of judgy folks out there. Because most people are going to judge, the most prominent thought is, "Am I sounding like I know what I'm talking about or do I sound like an idiot?" This feeling never goes away, no matter how many times one speaks in public.

Second lesson: because stage fright is not something that ever goes away, students, and even adults for that matter, don't defeat it; they can only adapt to it. They need to find things that calm themselves down. Some of the things you can suggest to them might be:

- Take deep breaths
- Visualize your success
- Think positive thoughts
- Converse with audience members
- Try power poses
- Practice your speech one more time
- Get something to drink
- Talk to a friend
- Do voice exercises
- Meditate

Whenever I am going to give a workshop or presentation, I arrive early enough at the venue, get the technology set up so I don't have to worry about it, and then walk around the building to stretch my legs. This always relaxes me and puts me more at ease. The key is for students to find what works for them. What is their way of calming themselves down?

> **TED TALK**
>
> *How I Beat Stage Fright by Joe Kowan*
> Here is a TED talk about how one speaker uses a particular strategy to overcome his case of stage fright.

Some people even go to extreme lengths to give themselves the courage to perform in front of others. Take this gentleman who created an entire song to give himself confidence to perform on stage:

It doesn't have to be to this level, but whatever works for students works for students. Help them find their Zen place by giving them 15 or so minutes to prepare before their speech to either go through their speech again, do some breathing exercises, or close their eyes for a few moments. During this time, you could play classical or meditative music.

One piece of advice that has been handed down through the ages to put a speaker at ease is to picture the audience members in their underwear or as naked. This advice has always perplexed me. I get the psychology of the audience having to be vulnerable just as you are, but it is still not a technique that I think would be helpful. Besides, you wouldn't want to see most people in their underwear, would you?

Third, as has already been stated, practice, practice, practice. Being prepared is probably the best way to work around stage fright. The reason is a prepared person feels more comfortable having run through it and knowing what to expect. Experience matters. What usually causes people to panic in situations is when things are unfamiliar to them. They have never experienced it before.

To train police officers not to panic when a dog is attacking them, they pad the person from head to toe and sic one of the K-9 units on them. After experiencing this a few times, the officer knows how to handle the situation. So when they are attacked on the job, their first instinct is not to panic but rather to react to the problem as they have experienced before. They can draw on their experiences to react in the proper way.

> **TODD TALK**
>
> To watch a video of Verlin explaining some of the things she uses to deal with stage fright that can be shown to students go to:
> https://www.youtube.com/watch?v=Z1xuvrDxN4E&t=8s
>
>

The more a student practices his speech, the more experience he gains. He can turn to this experience when something doesn't go as planned or when he feels his nerves setting in.

Some additional practical advice to consider

Two common mistakes I see students make when learning to publicly speak are talking too fast and, when they do make a mistake, actually calling themselves out about it. When the speech begins, their adrenaline is pumping, and the nervous energy is just bursting out of them. Without them even being aware of it, they begin to talk a mile a minute. I have seen it a thousand times, and because of this, it can be difficult to catch what they are talking about, and so the entire speech can become compromised. My advice is to tell students to slow themselves down to a pace where they almost feel they are talking too slowly. I am by nature a quick speaker. But working as a schoolteacher for nearly 30 years and having given hundreds of speeches, I have a different voice in those situations. I have learned to slow myself down because if I do not, I will speak too quickly.

There are several things you can do to remind your students to slow down, such as having them:

- Write "slow down" on a sticky note and place it where they are going to be speaking
- Plant a friend in the audience who gives them a signal should they be going too fast
- Make sure to pause when coming to the end of a sentence rather than blasting through to the next one. This allows the audience to catch up. We will talk about the power of the pause in a future chapter
- Put a symbol in their notes that serves as a reminder to slow down when starting
- Remember to breathe
- Read the audience. Do they look overwhelmed or unable to understand what is being said
- Set the pace. The average conversation is 150 words a minute. Mark on the written speech where 150 words is and try to make sure they don't reach that spot until a minute into the speech
- Try not to read. Besides the aforementioned reasons, we tend to read faster than we talk
- Repeat key points so that the audience can catch back up with what is being talked about
- Think of the presentation as step-by-step instructions or break it down into parts
- If using a slide deck, every time a new slide is moved to, make sure to pause for a moment to let the new slide sink in

The second piece of advice to give students is if anything does go wrong, and it almost always does, don't draw attention to it yourself. There is a great TED Talk by Simon Sinek on how good leaders inspire that I will use as an example when we get to our oratorical speech. At one point, the microphone he is using for the speech begins to buzz a little, so one of the tech guys gives him a new microphone that works better. Sinek does not even acknowledge the tech person nor the fact that he is switching microphones. He merely grabs the new one and continues on as though nothing has happened. When some of my students are watching this speech and I ask them about the switching of the microphone, they don't even recall it happening because it is such a seamless transition.

Things are going to go wrong in a speech. Someone's phone might go off, a baby could start to cry, the technology could fail, the wrong word might be used, or anything else that could go wrong will go wrong. The key is not to draw any attention to it. Keep in mind, when someone is giving a speech, the audience is not privy to the written speech. Thus, if a section gets skipped or something goes in the wrong order, they have no idea of this. They are just listening to what they are being told. I once worked with a student who would be giving his speech and would interrupt himself and lament about how he had screwed something up. At no point were we aware of this snafu until it was pointed out by the student. In fact, we probably would not have thought anything about it had he not said something.

Same thing goes with technology. I once gave a keynote with three other speakers. We each were given ten minutes to say our part before handing it off to the next person. I was the first to go, and I used every bit of the ten minutes, spinning tales and making inspiring statements. I turned it over to the next woman who wanted to show a video of the work she was doing with her students. She could not get the video to load and spent over half of her time trying to get it to work. The flow I had created with my own speech was completely stalled. She would have been better off simply skipping the video and going on with her speech. But the audience had to sit there uncomfortably with her as her anxiety grew more and more because she could not get it to work.

I cannot tell you how many times my PPT has closed for some unknown reason right in the middle of a talk. I don't stop, curse at the equipment, or make people wait a couple of minutes as I reopen the slide deck and try and find my place again. I just continue talking and calmly go over to my computer and bring up the slide deck again. Sure, people have noticed that my slides were no longer on display, but I didn't allow that to throw off the rhythm of my speech. They are still able to listen to my words even without the slide.

Part of having confidence is acting like you possess it even when you really don't. If you act like you know what you are talking about and continue through when things go wrong, people are going to follow you.

Shining a light

How you can shine a light on your students' performances is to make sure to give them effective feedback about how they did. In order to be effective, the feedback needs to be:

- Actionable – have you given them something they can specifically do?
  Example: Make sure you keep your head up when presenting and not look down all of the time.
- Specific/User-friendly – is the advice something they can point their finger at and either keep doing or change.
  Example: If you say the speech was not interesting, this is very abstract and difficult to figure out how to change. A more user-friendly version of this would be your speech was not engaging because you spoke in a monotone voice. That is something concrete that they can fix.
- Honest – there is a fine line that you walk with feedback. You don't want to crush a student's confidence, but you also don't want to inflate their ego under false pretenses.
  Example: instead of saying "you did a good job", which doesn't provide any useful feedback, you could say, "while there were positive elements to the speech, you were passionless. You need to figure out a way to express more enthusiasm with your voice".

- Goal-referenced – you have been teaching students the elements of a good speech and giving them goals to accomplish. Refer as much as possible to these goals.
Example: The focus of the speech was off because you did not stick to your throughline. You only said it once when it should be repeated several times.
- Given using descriptive language – the more specific you can be, the better the chance a student has to improve their work. The descriptive language not only lets the speaker know what was done well, but why it was effective.
Example: instead of saying, "I really liked your visuals", tell them I really liked the visual that showed the effects of polar ice caps. "That was really powerful".
- Non-judgmental – we want to evaluate the performance, not judge the content or student's opinion. Sometimes you will listen to speeches from people you do not agree with, but the point is not that they think the same as you; it is whether they communicated what they intended.
Example: If someone is giving a persuasive speech on why *The Shining* is an amazing book, and you say to them, *The Shining* isn't that great of a book, you have allowed your judgment to cloud your evaluation of the actual performance.
- Listening as well as talking – feedback should be a two-way conversation. It shouldn't just be you handing students back the rubric. It should be you talking with the student about the speech. I always try to have a five-minute conversation with students, asking them how they believe things went and then offering my own observations and insights. Then I listen to a goal they want to set for the next time.
Example: I thought your personal story about how you went to summer camp was very interesting. What did you think about your level of engagement with the audience?
- Timely – because you can evaluate the speech in real-time as it is happening, you should have feedback

ready to give. You just need to figure out how to do this in a timely fashion. If you wait too long, students might forget exactly what they did and not understand your comments. I usually try to schedule conferences with students no more than a day or two after their performance.

Example: I am going to have you get started on the next unit of study while I work my way around the students to have conversations about their speeches.

- Set them up for future success – the number one goal you should have when providing feedback for a student is not to judge them. That is what they most fear. Instead, you should be guiding them toward improvement and setting a goal. Each speech should be used as a game plan for how to make it better the next time.

Example: I noticed in your speech that you had a very short conclusion. In fact, it was a little abrupt. Remember that the conclusion is the last thing the audience is going to hear. How can you make that memorable? How can you leave them with something to think about such as a quote, a call to action, or a rhetorical question? Figure 5.1 shows what a rubric looks like that I return to students. Notice that in addition to merely circling the descriptions, I explain why I circled it. This WHY is the effective part of the feedback. If students do not know the why, they do not know how to continue doing something well or fix something that needs work.

> **TODD TALK**
>
> Here is a video on what effective feedback looks like to help you understand what it looks like when providing it to students:
>
> https://youtu.be/XsDriiTEc6E
>
>

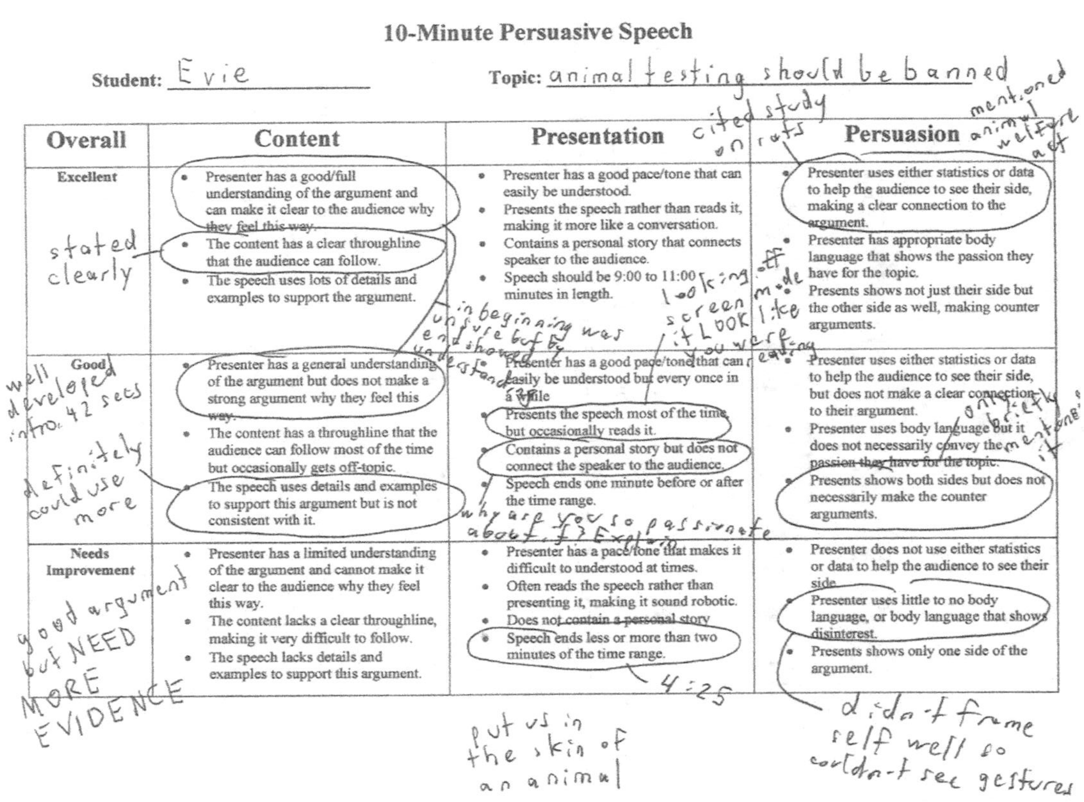

10-Minute Persuasive Speech

Student: Evie **Topic:** animal testing should be banned

Overall	Content	Presentation	Persuasion
Excellent	• Presenter has a good/full understanding of the argument and can make it clear to the audience why they feel this way. • The content has a clear throughline that the audience can follow. • The speech uses lots of details and examples to support the argument.	• Presenter has a good pace/tone that can easily be understood. • Presents the speech rather than reads it, making it more like a conversation. • Contains a personal story that connects speaker to the audience. • Speech should be 9:00 to 11:00 minutes in length.	• Presenter uses either statistics or data to help the audience to see their side, making a clear connection to the argument. • Presenter has appropriate body language that shows the passion they have for the topic. • Presents shows not just their side but the other side as well, making counter arguments.
Good	• Presenter has a general understanding of the argument but does not make a strong argument why they feel this way. • The content has a throughline that the audience can follow most of the time but occasionally gets off-topic. • The speech uses details and examples to support this argument but is not consistent with it.	• Presenter has a good pace/tone that can easily be understood but every once in a while • Presents the speech most of the time but occasionally reads it. • Contains a personal story but does not connect the speaker to the audience. • Speech ends one minute before or after the time range.	• Presenter uses either statistics or data to help the audience to see their side, but does not make a clear connection to their argument. • Presenter uses body language but it does not necessarily convey the passion they have for the topic. • Presents shows both sides but does not necessarily make the counter arguments.
Needs Improvement	• Presenter has a limited understanding of the argument and cannot make it clear to the audience why they feel this way. • The content lacks a clear throughline, making it very difficult to follow. • The speech lacks details and examples to support this argument.	• Presenter has a pace/tone that makes it difficult to understood at times. • Often reads the speech rather than presenting it, making it sound robotic. • Does not contain a personal story • Speech ends less or more than two minutes of the time range.	• Presenter does not use either statistics or data to help the audience to see their side. • Presenter uses little to no body language, or body language that shows disinterest. • Presents shows only one side of the argument.

stated clearly
well developed intro. 42 secs
definitely could use more
good argument but NEED MORE EVIDENCE
in beginning was unsure but by end showed understanding
cited study on rats
mentioned animal welfare act
looking off screen made it look like you were reading
why are you so passionate about it? Explain
only briefly mentioned it
4:25
put us in the skin of an animal
didn't frame self well so couldn't see gestures

FIGURE 5.1

6

Expository – the five-minute TED-Ed speech

A good next stepping-stone speech for students to attempt is the five-minute expository TED-Ed speech. There are four reasons why it is good to begin the first formal speech with this particular one:

1. Its length
   Five minutes seems completely attainable. If you want to build up the endurance of your students, you need to start small. If you asked students to begin with a 20-minute speech, they would think that is unattainable. Five minutes seems doable. Then, when you ask them to do a ten-minute speech, it doesn't seem so impossible, and then they work their way up to the 20-minute TED Talk.
2. Its purpose
   An expository speech is merely providing information for the audience. There is no argument to be made, no comparison to draw, and no motive to inspire. The speaker is simply relaying information about a topic they care about. This could be a book they enjoy, a singer they like, a sport they play, or a topic that fascinates them. It is very unassuming but still requires students to give enough information so that the audience understands what they are being informed about. The speech

can't have gaps in the narrative, so students must determine the details and examples needed to make their story clear.

3. Its focus

    When students are learning public speaking, there are a lot of things to consider. However, if you try to teach them all at once, you are going to overwhelm your students. This speech is only asking students to focus on their voice, which is just one aspect of giving a speech. A common mistake novices make when giving a speech is that they read it. And they read it in a monotone manner, which makes it sound lifeless and without any emotion. By allowing students to focus on their voice, they can concentrate on giving the speech with some feeling. This is extremely important in making a connection with the audience. I often say, if it doesn't sound like you care about your speech, why should the audience care? Focusing on putting emotion into their voice will help to demonstrate this.

4. Its format

    The five-minute speech will be using the format of the TED-Ed Talk. This is a bit less intimidating than the TED Talk speech. A TED Talk has a presenter standing on a stage, usually on a round red carpet, and the focus is on them. This can be a lot of pressure on someone. The TED-Ed Talk format takes this pressure off because the focus is solely on the visuals.

> **TED-ED TALK**
>
> *The World's Most Mysterious Book by Stephen Bax* is a TED-Ed Talk about a mysterious book known as the *Voynich Manuscript*.
>
> *How Tsunamis Work by Alex Gendler* is a teaching about what a tsunami is.
>
> *A Brie(f) History of Cheese by Paul S. Kindstedt* is a brief history of cheese.
>
> *The Best Way to Apologize (According to Science)* is about how you say you are sorry.
>
> *3 Tips on How to Study Effectively* are a talk on how to study effectively.

What is a TED-Ed Talk

A TED-Ed Talk is a five-minute lesson. It is typically animated, so you do not even see who is narrating the action. All you hear is a voice. And this voice must bring life to what is happening in the animation, meaning it must be animated as well.

Here is an example of a few TED-Ed Talks:

By having students give their first formal speech as a TED-Ed Talk, they do not have to worry about the audience looking at them and can instead focus on narrating their speech.

Since your students are most likely not experts on animation, they will be creating a simple slidedeck for PowerPoint, Google Slides, Prezi, or whichever platform they feel comfortable with. Then they will narrate the visuals in the slide deck to give their speech.

Writing of the speech

There are two schools of thought when it comes to the writing of a speech. School #1 is that every word should be written out that is going to be spoken. One of the biggest advantages of this approach is that the speech is consistent every time, from the practice to the final product. The speaker might wordsmith or edit parts of it that do not sound as good in practice, but what is on the paper is what is going to be spoken. This way, nothing gets forgotten or details don't get left out. The disadvantage is that when something is written out word for word, the tendency is to want to read those words, and when people read, they sound like robots.

School #2 is that the speaker simply outlines the important parts of the speech and then expands on those when talking. Every word is not as important as the collection of ideas. The advantage of this is that organically the presentation becomes more of a conversation because every word is not being read. It is easier to set the correct tone in this manner. The disadvantage is that it is easier for the speaker to get side-tracked and lose sight of the throughline because the script is not focusing on every word.

There is no right or wrong; there is what works for each of your students as a speaker. You can choose to teach one of these methods, but I give students a choice in which one works best for them.

I personally prefer the outline method, and I learned this from being a teacher for many years. When I first began as a teacher, I would write out a script of what I was going to say to students, word for word. This is a script I took from my lesson on perspectives in history:

- There are many times there is more than one perspective in history because usually history involves more than one person and everyone has different perspectives.
  - When people think of history, they sometimes think of dates and names placed in a textbook that we memorize and regurgitate back up when test time comes. But history is much more subjective than you think.
  - For example, let's say you and your sibling are playing in the house and trying to pass a football back and forth. Your sibling throws you the ball, but you miss it and it breaks a lamp. You both go running off to your mother to explain what happened.
    - What story are you going to tell your mother?
    - What story is your sibling going to tell?
    - Who is right?
    - You both are, and you're both wrong. History has many sides to a story, and thus history can be looked at from many different perspectives.
  - Because of these various sides, history is not really written in stone as you might think. There are arguments and debates over what really happened in many different situations.
  - We are going to look at some of the more controversial moments in history where almost no one agrees or can figure out what happened in these situations.

I would print this out and have it on my desk in front of me, and I would go through it word by word. One thing I noticed, though, after doing this for five classes a day for three years, was that I stopped reading from the script and merely presented the lesson. I was familiar enough with it that I did not need the script as a crutch. And I might change things to suit the class. Instead of telling the story of throwing a football back and forth with a sibling, which might leave out some who do not have siblings or who do not like football, I might change the story to a situation where you get into an argument with your parents about who ate the last donut left on the counter.

Now that I have more experience, my lesson plans are more concise and commonly fit on a sticky note. The same lesson would look something like this:

- History is more than facts and dates
- All about perspective
- Story of football or donut?
- Can anyone think of controversial events in history?

Of course, this took many years of being a teacher and becoming more comfortable in that role to be able to switch from the script to the outline.

Most of your students will want to write it all out because they are new to this process. I always tell them a five-minute speech will typically be around 750 words. You could give them a graphic organizer such as this to organize their thoughts:

Outline for TED-Ed Talk
(typically around 750 words)

My topic:

Introduction

Why am I informing you of this?

Throughline:

Body – break your speech into clear steps that you explain

Idea 1:

Supporting details/examples

What is a visual you could use that would support and enhance what it is you are talking about?

Idea 2:

Supporting details/examples/visuals:

What is a visual you could use that would support and enhance what it is you are talking about?

Idea 3:

Supporting details/examples/visuals:

> What is a visual you could use that would support and enhance what it is you are talking about?

Add ideas should you need it

Conclusion

> What should your audience have learned from you and why is it important?
>
> Review the main points:
>
> Closing statement:

This graphic organizer provides the structure for the speech to make sure nothing is left out that needs to be included. This graphic organizer can be printed from https://www.thegiftedguy.com/public-speaking.

Whichever method students choose to use, I always stress the importance of a rehearsal to find all of the clunky words and phrases as well as to determine the timing of the speech. This revision process is where the bulk of the work for the speech takes place and is often the difference between a good and a bad speech.

Creating a good slidedeck

For this first formal speech, I like the use of a slidedeck for three reasons:

1. It gives them support for their speech. Instead of having to memorize it, they can use the slides as an outline and a guide to what they will be saying. Of course, you will need to remind them over and over not to read the slides
2. The audience will be compelled to look at the slides, so it takes the focus off of the speaker and provides a little break from being judged. The speaker can relax a little
3. Another form of communication is the use of a slidedeck. Many TED speakers use a slidedeck when speaking, although some do not. However, given that an audience has both visual and auditory learners, providing meaningful visuals to illustrate your points strengthens the communication piece

There are certain guidelines anyone should follow for an effective speaking slide deck. Otherwise, speakers tend to simply cut and paste their actual speech onto the slide. This causes them to a) read the slide (reading is always bad), b) make the slide too busy and thus actually take away from the visual aspect of it, and c) insult the intelligence of the audience. We may assume an audience is always ignorant, but we don't want to extend this to thinking they are illiterate. I always assume that my audience can read, and I fully expect them to read what is up there. If you have the text all written out, they are not listening to you at all but are merely reading the script you have provided for them.

Here is a PPT I used early in my teaching career:

  COINS

$ Most early cultures traded precious metals. In 2500 B.C. the Egyptians produced metal rings for use as money. The Ancient Greeks used iron rods to represent money. By 700 B.C., a group of seafaring people called the Lydians became the first in the Western world to make coins. The Lydians used coins to expand their vast trading empire. The Greeks and Romans continued the coining tradition and passed it on to later Western civilizations. Coins were appealing since they were durable, easy to carry and contained valuable metals.

FIGURE 6.1

You can see there are several issues here when it comes to a presentation slide:

1) The text is all written out in one lump sum. It would be difficult for anyone to extrapolate terms or ideas because it all sort of runs together
2) The font, while fancy, is not very easy to read. A simpler font that can be clearly seen would be best
3) The visuals are not of good resolution and thus difficult to see
4) It is not very colorful or eye catching. Pretty boring in fact
5) Worst sin of all, the title gives the topic but not the throughline

> **YOUTUBE VIDEO**
>
> Here is a comedian giving practical advice for slidedecks and what you should definitely not do:
> *Life After Death by Powerpoint (Corporate Comedy Video) by Don McMillan*: https://www.youtube.com/watch?v=KbSPPFYxx3o

There are certain guidelines students should follow when creating a slide. First and foremost, the point is that it adds meaningful content to your presentation.

Guidelines for a TED-worthy slide deck

- Incorporate visuals that add something (content or depth) to your presentation
- Find high resolution visuals
- Make sure folks can clearly see the visuals
- Use bullet points to separate the main ideas but do not overuse them
- Never have sentences longer than a couple of lines unless you are using a lengthy quote
- Don't need a slide for everything
- Slides also don't cost a thing, so feel free to spread information over a few slides instead of cramming it onto one
- Font needs to be of a size and style to be able to read easily
- Don't get bogged down by slide transitions or animation. Especially avoid typewriter, whip, and drop down, which puts words on the screen letter-by-letter and brings the rhythm of your speech to a halt
- KISS – Keep It Super Simple

A better version of the slide would look like this:

COINS MADE IT EASIER
- Most early cultures traded precious metals
  - 2500 B.C. Egyptians produced metal rings
  - Ancient Greeks used iron rods for money
- Lydian made 1st coins 700 B.C.

FIGURE 6.2

- Greeks and Romans passed it on to Western civilizations
    - Appeal
    - Durable
    - Easy to carry
    - Contained valuable metals

FIGURE 6.3

Let's see if it took care of all of the problems from before:

1) The text is all written out in one lump sum. It would be difficult for anyone to extrapolate terms or ideas because it all sort of runs together.
    - ♦ The text is now broken up into bullet points to make it easier to read
2) The font, while fancy, is not very easy to read. A simpler font that can be clearly seen would be better
    - ♦ Changed to an easy-to-read Times New Roman. Not fancy but easy to see
3) The visuals are not of good resolution and thus difficult to see
    - ♦ Visuals are larger and of higher resolution, allowing details to be seen more clearly
4) It is not very colorful or eye catching. Pretty boring, in fact
    - ♦ A colorful border was added to give it some flourish
5) Worst sin of all, the title gives the topic but not the throughline
    - ♦ The point of the slides is now in the title, which is that coins made trading easier

Notice also that the information is now spread out across two slides rather than crammed onto one.

> **TED TALK**
>
> *Are Athletes Really Getting Faster, Better, Stronger? By David Epstein*
> A video with an effective slidedeck that is used to express ideas.

Providing a rubric as a guiding point

Now that students have begun to write the speech and prepare the visuals, they need to know what the expectations are. This can all be accomplished by either giving them a rubric or creating one together. Either way, the rubric needs to lay out what it looks like for a student who has successfully accomplished the skills you have determined for the first speech.

The requirements of the speech were:

- The voice
- The time length
- The throughline
- The visuals

Each can become its own category but then whoever is creating the rubric needs to break each action down into a few parts. After all, there are several factors that make a successful voice, including:

- Pace
- Tone
- Fluency

A student could use excellent pace and tone but use a lot of *ums* and *likes* or other such filler words. She might be fluent and speak at an easy to understand speed, but she might sound like a robot. Or he might speak clearly and with inflection, but it is so fast it is difficult to keep up. It is the combination of these pieces that gives us the finished puzzle of what the voice sounded like.

These need to be broken down also because a student needs to be able to use the rubric to pinpoint what can be worked on the next time. If the rubric merely says:

Student speaks with fluency at an easy-to-understand pace and shows emotion.

And the evaluator indicates that this was good but not excellent, the student is not sure which factor prevented his voice from being excellent. Having it broken down into smaller pieces allows a student to pinpoint what he did well and should continue to do or what he can work on for the next speech.

Figure 6.4 shows what a completed rubric could look like.

Notice it uses the categories discussed before of *visuals* and *throughline*. It combined the voice and time into a single category titled *presentation*. If you would like a copy of this rubric to use with your students, one can be found at https://www.thegiftedguy.com/public-speaking.

Whether you decide to make the rubric yourself or collaborate with students on it, the number one rule of making a rubric is that your descriptions need to show, not tell. I have seen many rubrics describe the following:

- Student is completely prepared
- Student is pretty prepared
- Student is somewhat prepared
- Student is not prepared

These adverbs do not paint a very detailed picture. They are too general and, as a result, can be interpreted in many different ways. Instead of merely stating the preparedness, show what it looks like:

- The student has everything that is needed for the presentation, and it appears that the speech has been rehearsed
- The student either does not have everything that is needed to give the speech or the speech does not appear to be rehearsed
- The student neither has everything needed for the speech, nor does it does not appear as though it were rehearsed
- Student is missing major items needed for the speech, causing it to lose effectiveness, or is simply not ready to give the speech

5-Minute TED Ed Talk

Student: _____ Topic: _____

Overall	Presentation	Visuals	Throughline
Excellent	• Speaks fluently, avoids too many ums and likes. • The pace is appropriate to what is being talked about but always allows the audience to understand the speaker clearly. • Presents rather than reads, doesn't sound monotone. • The speech should be between 4:30 – 5:30 minutes in length.	• Has just one idea per slide. • There are more than 5 visuals used in the presentation. • The visuals add to the content of the speech by providing additional information or demonstrating a point the speaker is making.	• What is being talked about connects to your throughline. • The throughline is clearly stated throughout the entire speech • Speech has a clear beginning, middle, and end that are divided appropriately amongst the time.
Good	• Speaks fluently but has a few too many ums and likes. • The pace is appropriate to what is being talked about but sometimes gets too fast or too slow. • Presents rather than reads for most of the speech but occasionally sounds monotone. • The speech is slightly before or after the 4:30 – 5:30 minute window.	• At times contains more than one idea per slide. • There are 5 visuals used in the presentation. • The visuals add to the content of the speech most of the time by providing additional information or demonstrating a point the speaker is making, but sometimes a visual does not add anything.	• What is being talked about mostly connects to your throughline but every once in a while gets sidetracked. • The throughline is stated a couple of times during the speech but needs to be more. • Speech has a beginning, middle, and end but are either not divided appropriately amongst the time or are difficult to tell when transitioned.
Needs Improvement	• Does not speaks fluently, many ums and likes that distract the audience. • The pace is not appropriate, either going too fast for the audience to catch up or too slow so that it becomes a distraction. • Reads most of the speech in a monotone, causing it to sound flat. • The speech is more than a minute before or after the 4:30 – 5:30 minute window.	• Too many ideas on a single slide, causing confusion to the audience. • There are less than 5 visuals used in the presentation. • The visuals do not add to the content of the speech, merely acting as placeholders than giving additional content.	• Often times what is being talked about does not connect to your throughline. • The throughline is not clearly stated, causing the audience to wonder what it is about. • Speech does not have a beginning, middle, and end.

FIGURE 6.4

This is the difference between showing and telling, and it is a big difference. There is very little interpretation needed by the evaluator because the description clearly shows what it should look like.

If you would like some further tips on how to create an effective and objective rubric, you can watch this TODD Talk:

> **TODD TALK**
>
> Here is a video explaining how to create a rubric that you can use to make your rubrics, or if you plan on having students help with the creation of the rubrics, you can show to them:
>
> https://youtu.be/H_eGyATb4JA
>
>

This rubric, in addition to being used to evaluate students after the fact, can be used beforehand by them as a blueprint of what they need to do. I give students the rubric before they begin to work on the speech because it can help to guide them in their work. If they are preparing their speech for the actual performance, they can go through the rubric to make sure they have all of the required elements as well as check to make sure they are performed at a high quality.

One of the biggest problems I have with my own students is that they do not know how to use a rubric properly. This not only applies to my elementary and middle school kids, but also to my high school and graduate school adults. I give them a rubric that clearly lays out what they need to do in order to receive high marks for an assignment, and I receive their work full of gaps and mistakes that could have been fixed had the students simply gone through it with the rubric before turning it in.

After several years of frustration from having my students complain about being marked down for things blatantly stated in the rubric, I made this video to watch before we began to work with it in order to help in their use:

Shining a light

> **TODD TALK**
>
> Here is a video explaining to students how to read a rubric and use it to help them make their work being evaluated better:
> https://youtu.be/xLChSaYruFA
>
>

A five-minute TED-Ed Talk is an unassuming way for students to be introduced to public speaking. It puts the spotlight on the slide-deck rather than the speaker, and students can simply focus on getting the words out. There are a lot of moving parts to giving a speech, and to try to focus on all of them at once would be overwhelming to even the most confident of children.

When I am teaching young children how to play tennis, I do not show them how to hit a forehand, a backhand, a serve, a volley, an overhead, or a lob all at once, even though these are all important parts of the game of tennis. I take these one step at a time, usually starting with the volley because it is the easiest one, and letting the player develop this skill before moving on to a more challenging one. This is the same approach I take with beginning public speakers. If we want them to have confidence, we need to build this in them piece by piece.

The first and easiest part is the voice. Here are five things to remind students to consider when making sure their voice is heard clearly:

1. Inflection – is there variance in the pitch of your voice in how you deliver a word? You bring life to its pronunciation.
2. Pace – does the speed of your delivery do two things: 1) allow the audience to follow without getting left behind, and 2) do you alter it to fit the tone of your speech?
3. Volume – are you loud enough is the first aspect of this. But more subtle is do you vary this volume to fit the mood you

are creating with the speech? Variance of volume can have desired effects on your audience.
4. Articulation – are you pronouncing the words correctly? Because the goal of the speech is communication, using simpler words instead of advanced vocabulary that might leave some audience members confused is important. Also, even if you are not sure of a word, articulate it with confidence and people will accept that this is way it is pronounced. If your words run together, it is going to be difficult for the audience to understand you so you need to have distinctive spaces between them.
5. Rhythm – one thing that people often overlook is that grammar acts as a guide to the rhythm of your speech. For example:

, = slight pause
; = longer pause for effect
. = hard pause
- = brief pause for effect
" = cue to separate out

This rhythm needs to occur in your spoken words as well. People should feel the commas, should experience the period, understand you are quoting something. This rhythm is what makes the speech seem presented rather than read. Pauses can be just as if not more powerful than speaking words. They certainly can create an effect.

TODD TALK

To watch a video explaining the five things to consider regarding voice that you can show to students, go here:
https://www.youtube.com/watch?v=FDHlxJchwpM

7

Demonstrative – the ten-minute speech

In an effort to build up the endurance of speaking, the next speech you should assign would be the ten-minute one. This requires students to speak for twice as long as they did for the five-minute, but this does not seem unattainable. This chapter will provide an outline for how to teach the ten-minute demonstrative speech.

Chance for reflection

Before beginning the next speech, though, this is a great opportunity for students to reflect upon their five-minute one. They may have done this a little if you have conferenced with them. But it is always good to put students into as many risk-free, non-judgmental situations in order to practice their public speaking ability. Not only that, by stating a goal of what they will be working on for the next speech, it gives them something to work toward.

Much like homework, practice speeches should be used solely for the purpose of practicing something. I usually do not give a time limit, nor do I provide feedback. I want students to get as comfortable as they can in front of the classroom, and the more times they do this, the quicker this occurs. Just as band students

DOI: 10.4324/9781003385981-8

go to the practice room to get all the squeaks, blats, and sour notes worked out, so too should you allow your students to make mistakes and not draw attention to them. Reserve your effective feedback for the formal speeches, much like the band students hear an assessment of the concert they have been a part of and were working up to.

Practice opportunity

Have students give a speech in which they reflect on their five-minute TED-Ed Talk.

- What went well?
- What could be improved?
- What is a goal you have for next time?

Have students determine something specific they want to work on in this speech and then work toward that goal. Some common goals from the previous speech might be:

- Make sure to speak at an understandable pace
- Speak with emotion in your voice
- Try making eye contact with the audience
- Avoid ums, like, and other fillers
- Have a developed opening and closing

Any time there might be a chance to have students speaking, you should offer it if time allows.

Requirements for demonstrative speech

The next speech I typically have students do is the demonstrative speech. The rationale behind this is threefold: 1) it allows students to be experts on something, which is what one has to do many times in a speech; 2) they have to explain their expertise in language that others who are not experts are able to understand; 3) it forces them to focus on details.

Some things in this speech remain the same as the previous speech. Speakers should still:

- Focus on the throughline
- Have a clear beginning, middle, and end
- Make sure to have emotion in their voices and not sound like a robot
- Use of visuals, although these can be demonstrations as well

New layers are being added, though:

- Purpose must be to teach or demonstrate how to do something
- Must be ten minutes in length
- Need to make appropriate eye contact with the audience

Students no longer have the safety net of just being a voice. Now they are bodies as well and so everything from their posture to their eye contact will be observed.

The rubric in Figure 7.1 reflects the changes to the speech and should be given to students as you explain these new requirements so that students are aware of the additions.

This rubric can be printed from https://www.thegiftedguy.com/public-speaking.

How does one teach something?

Essentially when students are giving a demonstrative speech, they are teaching the audience something: some knowledge, some skill, some idea, or some talent that they possess. They are trying to show someone else how to do this. Cooking shows are a great example of this. Their goal is to teach the audience how to make the food they are cooking. An indication of success would be that, by the end of the show, anyone watching would have

Demonstrative – the ten-minute speech ◆ 93

10-Minute Demonstrative Speech Rubric

Student _____ Topic _____

Overall	Speaking	Clarity/Details	Visuals
Excellent	• Speaks fluently, does not say like or um too much. • Makes consistent eye contact with audience, not looking down or off into space. • Varying tones are used throughout that give the speech life and emotion to what speaker is trying to convey to the audience. • Speech should be 9:00 to 11:00 minutes in length.	• Speech informs and teaches someone something and teaches someone should be able to do it by the end. • Topic is broken down into clear, detailed steps. • Stays on the topic of what is being taught, mentions throughline several times throughout the speech. • Transition words used to make sure audience is on the right track.	• Main point explained for all visuals by the speaker, adding to its effectiveness. • Visuals are used that add depth to the topic and helps the audience in their understanding of what is being taught. • Visuals are used consistently whenever something new is being introduced or would help in the explanation of what is being taught.
Good	• Speaks fluently most of the speech, only saying like or um a few times. • Makes eye contact most of the time, but there are long stretches of time where no eye contact is made. • Varying tones are used that give the speech life and emotion to what speaker is trying to convey to the audience, but at times is flat and/or monotone. • Speech should be no more than a minute under 9:00 or over 11:00 in length	• Speech informs and teaches someone something but not completely, a detail or step is left out. • Topic is broken down into steps but not always explained in detail or clearly. • Stays on the topic of what is being taught, mentions throughline from time to time throughout the speech. • Times where transition words are used to make sure audience is on the right track but occasionally get lost.	• Main point of most visuals is explained by the speaker, adding to its effectiveness but some not. • Most visuals that are used that add depth to the topic and helps the audience in their understanding of what is being taught, but a couple are off-topic or distracting. • Visuals are used most times whenever something new is being introduced or a visual would help in the explanation of what is being taught, but spots where one would have been helpful.
Needs Improvement	• Does not speak fluently, says like or um too much. • Little or no eye contact is made, majority of the time spent looking elsewhere. • Monotone is used that makes the speaker sound robotic and does not convey emotion. • Speech is well under 9:00 or over 11:00 minutes in length.	• Speech does not inform and/or teach someone something, audience is left confused as to how to do what is being taught. • Topic is broken down into clear, detailed steps. • Stays on the topic of what is being taught, mentions throughline several times throughout the speech. • Transition words not used very often to make sure audience is on the right track, causing them to get lost.	• Main point of the visual is not explained by the speaker, adding confusion. • Visuals used do not add depth to the topic or not used at all. • Visuals are not used consistently whenever something new is being introduced or would help in the explanation of what is being taught.

FIGURE 7.1

the confidence to prepare this meal. In order to do this, the chef needs to give every step of the process. If he forgets a step, the food will not turn out as planned.

Imagine a chef showing how to make chicken parmesan. She skips the step of flattening the chicken before cooking. This in turn causes the chicken not to cook all the way through in the pan or, in trying to cook it all the way through, it ends up burning the outside. Either way the dish is ruined because that step was not addressed.

Another way to look at it is if you are teaching a student how to solve a math problem. You have to use the order of operations, which has been turned into the acronym PEMDAS. These are the steps you must go through a solve a problem and the order you must do them in:

- Parenthesis
- Exponents
- Multiply
- Divide
- Add
- Subtract

If you are going to do the following problem:

$$8 + 7 \times 5 =$$

Following the order in which the question is written, the process would be:

$$8 + 7 = 15$$
$$15 \times 5 = 75$$
$$\text{Answer: } 75$$

However, if you follow PEMDAS, the problem would be solved like this:

$$7 \times 5 = 35$$
$$8 + 35 = 43$$

Answer: 43

Those are two very different answers. Knowing this detail of PEMDAS changes the answer. If someone were to use the wrong method, they would get the incorrect answer.

When teaching something in a speech, your students have to make sure they are including all of the steps. Can the audience do what is being shown to them with the information provided?

Take, for instance, this video on how to do a backflip: https://www.youtube.com/watch?v=ltho8_PzC2U. The video is five minutes in length, and the question I always ask students after watching it is whether they think they can now do a backflip. The answer is always a resounding no. This is not because the task is so difficult, though. This is because the person teaching this skill leaves out so many steps and details.

He starts out the video by saying that you have to focus. Then he follows it up with the prerequisites of knowing how to do a bridge stretch and a back roll, as well as a recommendation of being in general good shape. None of these are clearly defined or explained, so I cannot do what he is asking me to do. Focus on what? What does that look like? What indicates success?

But watch this video on juggling created by me:

https://www.youtube.com/watch?v=Mokt-vqr34A_.

It is also a difficult skill to ask of people, but when I ask students after watching it, they seem to have a lot more confidence in accomplishing this task. The difference they voice is that I break my task down into five clear steps and then explain each of the steps in detail. The backflip video was too general and did not explain how to do the complicated things he was asking.

In an effort to KISS, you need to break whatever you are teaching down into clearly defined steps. Each of those steps needs to be explained in such a way that the audience knows what you are talking about.

Language of the audience

By having students become the experts for this speech, they must explain it to folks who are not. That is what TED is all about: gathering the greatest minds in the world and getting them to explain to others who may not have the same understanding as them. Take, for example, this TED Talk by Vilayanur Ramachandran, who is the director of the Center for Brain and Cognition at the University of California, San Diego:

> **TED TALK**
>
> *3 Clues to Understanding Your Brain by V.S. Ramachandran* is a TED Talk that discusses something very complicated in language easier to understand.

He obviously knows a lot about the brain, but his audience doesn't. So he has to explain it in such a way that they do.

In order to be able to teach something, it needs to be broken down into understandable chunks. And then these chunks need to be explained in a way that people who know nothing about the subject can comprehend. This really forces speakers to focus on the details and speak in a language that everyone can decipher. It is almost like they are translating their language so that others can understand. In the TED Talk *Talk Nerdy to Me*, Melissa Marshall explains how, when working with engineers with their big

> **TED TALK**
>
> In the TED Talk entitled *Talk Nerdy to Me* by Melissa Marshall, the speaker talks about how engineers need to talk in the language of non-engineers.

brains, she had to teach them how to talk in the language of non-engineers in order to get their ideas across to others.

This is just one example of how you cannot assume people know how to speak the language you normally use in your field of expertise, whether it be sports, a profession, a skill, or the like. Find a common language others can understand and give your speech in that.

Breaking it into steps

You know that as a teacher when explaining something you need to break it down into smaller pieces. Otherwise it will be too difficult to swallow. It is sort of like someone trying to take a 12 ounce steak and put the whole thing in their mouth. He has to cut it up into smaller pieces that he can chew properly and then digest. The same goes for your lessons. If you try to teach the end result without chunking it, it becomes a very daunting task, and your students are just going to choke on it. You need to apply this same idea to your students while creating their demonstration speeches. They will need to break down what it is they are teaching into smaller parts.

Take the simple act of making toast. If someone is teaching another person how to make toast, she doesn't just say "cook the bread until it becomes crisp". She must walk the person through each of the steps that lead up to bread becoming toast. Here is a TED Talk that discusses this very thing:

The video mentions the idea of nodes and links. Nodes are the actual actions you must perform. The link is how each action connects to the next which will result in the desired outcome. There is a flow to these links and nodes. Node #4 has to connect to node #5. If they are not linked, there is a gap in the lesson, and those listening will not know where to go next.

> **TED TALK**
>
> *Got a Wicked Problem? First, Tell Me How You Make Toast by Tom Wujec* is a TED Talk that discusses how things can be broken down into parts.

STUDENT ACTIVITY

Give individual students or a group of students a simple act they need to teach to the class. They must assume the audience is ignorant and knows nothing about the skill. Every step must be taught and explained. Some skills to consider:

- Tying shoelace
- Putting on a shirt
- Catching a ball
- Using a pencil
- Making a phone call
- Drinking a glass of water
- Riding a bike
- Sharpening your pencil
- Coloring a coloring page
- Brushing your hair

As an example, you and the class can break down together how to brush your teeth. First, challenge them to write down the steps themselves, then go through as a class and see what was left out or not addressed.

Here is a fairly detailed list of steps one takes in brushing teeth:

1. Getting the toothbrush
2. Holding the toothbrush by the handle, away from the bristles
3. Putting water on the brush
4. Opening the toothpaste
5. Squeezing an eyebrow-length of toothpaste onto the bristles
6. Putting the cap back on the toothpaste
7. Opening mouth and applying a little pressure, brushing the bristles across the teeth, starting with the back top, working all the way around, then moving to the bottom
8. Every 30 seconds or so, spitting toothpaste out and not swallowing
9. Brushing teeth for a total of two minutes
10. Rinsing off the toothbrush
11. Rapping the toothbrush on the side of the sink to get rid of excess water
12. Rinsing your mouth with water but not swallowing
13. Spitting out water into the sink

> 14. Wiping your mouth on a towel
> 15. Putting toothbrush and toothpaste away
> 16. Cleaning the sink
>
> Use the opportunities students might leave out as examples of what happens when they do not provide all of the details.
>
> For example, nearly everyone forgets to explain that you shouldn't swallow the toothpaste. They think that this is just a given and people know not to do that. On the contrary, it is one of the most important rules of brushing your teeth and it is important to make sure it is followed. Or when you say "spit out the toothpaste", does this mean you spit it out anywhere, like all over the bathroom mirror? The detail of spitting it into the sink is very important. Talk about the consequences of skipping a step and what might happen. How can skipping a step throw off the rest of the sequence?

Students will need to break down into steps all the actions one would have to take in order to accomplish the task they are asking of their audience. These details are very important, and the omission of any of them might result in a failure of communication.

Importance of transitions

Because the speech is being broken down into steps, transitions between these need to be very clear so that the audience can follow the links between the nodes. They should think of themselves as a tour guide. When a tour guide is giving a tour, she doesn't just run over to something or go anywhere without letting the tourists know what she is doing. She directs them, "OK, now we are going over here", and then she explains what they are looking at. "Now follow me in this direction", and the crowd comes along obediently, able to keep up because her commands are so clear. The same goes for an audience. The speaker is taking them on a tour and thus needs to make sure to let them know where they are going next through the use of transition words.

One of the simplest ways to create transitions is simply to number the steps. It might sound something like this:

> Here are the seven steps for how to fold a paper airplane.

Then you simply announce the number of the step you are talking about:

> Step number one, you take the piece of paper and fold it hotdog style rather than hamburger. This means you fold it vertically rather than horizontally.

When you have explained the step and are moving on to the next, you simply announce that number as well:

> Step number two has you turning the paper so that it is horizontal and grabbing the corner of the open edge of the folded paper. You pull the corner down until it creates a triangle, making sure it is flush with the bottom of the piece of paper.

You continue this throughout all seven steps, announcing every time you begin a new one.

Sometimes you will not have numbered steps. You can still use transition words to let the audience know when you have moved to different sections of the speech. Some transition words that are useful are:

- To begin
- My first point is …
- My next point is …
- Next
- Following this
- After that
- Then
- Therefore
- In conclusion
- Given these points
- To sum up
- Finally
- I would like to end with this thought
- Overall it might be said

Keep in mind, the speaker is leading people through the speech. Giving them as much guidance as possible is just going to make it easier for them to follow along. The obvious places students will want to have transitions are at the beginning, into the main part of the speech, and when they get to the conclusion. But there can be transitions in additional places to make the progression of the speech much more clear:

> **TODD TALK**
>
> Here are some examples of transitions between sections of a speech and when they should be used, that can be shown to students:
> https://youtu.be/Mw98UPPUsLE
>
>

Making sure visuals communicate what they intend to?

Although I talked about visuals in the last chapter, I am going to mention them again here because they can bring so much to a speech. The visuals need to not only be present; you need to teach students to choose visuals that add to the effectiveness of the communication of their speech. This is because a visual can communicate so much. Amy Herman talks about what she trains people to look for when teaching visual intelligence:

> **TED TALK**
>
> *A Lesson on Looking by Amy Herman* is a TED Talk that discusses how things can be broken down into parts.

She breaks it down into four parts, which you can discuss with your students when they are looking for their own visuals:

- Assess
- Analyze
- Articulate
- Act

Students need to make sure to choose visuals that communicate what they want them to. For a little help with this, you can show them the following TODD Talk.

Visuals are not always images

Visuals do not need to be limited to images in a slide deck either. Visuals come in all forms such as a clip from a video, a drawing, or a live demonstration. Take, for instance, this TED Talk where Fabian Oefner shows how he created some pretty amazing visuals by combining them with science:

> **TODD TALK**
>
> To show a video on making sure your visuals communicate what they want them to, go to:
>
> https://youtu.be/hAUAJ9rYuCQ
>
>

> **TED TALK**
>
> *Psychedelic Science by Fabian Oefner* is a TED Talk with amazing demonstration visuals.

I show this speech to students to demonstrate to them how amazing visuals can be, but also to show them that even the greatest visuals can't save a poor speech. The speech is delivered in such a flat way that there is no connection made between the speaker and the audience. The audience cannot even tell when he is telling a joke, and when he finishes the speech, the audience is silent because they are not even aware it is over. I use this as a lesson to emphasize that it is important to convey emotions about your visuals to set a tone.

I counter the talk with this one:

> **TED TALK**
>
> *The Thrilling Potential of SixthSense Technology by Pranav Mistry* is another speech that not only uses visuals very well, but is also presented in a very engaging manner.

In this speech, the speaker uses video clips very effectively, but he also speaks with such enthusiasm and shows such passion for his topic with his body language that the audience cannot help but connect with him. They are practically hanging on his every word as he explains the amazing technology he has created and explains so well using his words combined with the visuals.

For a demonstration speech, students will have to determine the best way to show what they are teaching. For example, if someone is showing the audience how to swim, she might need to show a video because it would be difficult to do this live since there is no access to a pool. If someone is teaching how to make an origami animal, images that show each of the steps might be an effective way to go since each step is so precise and detailed. If someone is explaining how to do a math problem, a live demonstration using the board might be an applicable way.

Students should be giving as much thought and consideration to their visuals as they do to the content they are creating for their speech. Each of these work together to do the communication.

The demonstrative speech

Now that students know what needs to go into their demonstrative speech, they need to plan it out and fill in the details. They can use this graphic organizer for doing this:

Outline for demonstrative speech
(1,500 words = approximately ten minutes)

My topic:

Introduction

Why am I teaching you this:

Throughline:

Body – break your lesson down into clear steps which you explain.

Step 1:

Supporting details/examples/visuals:

Step 2:

Supporting details/examples/visuals:

Step 3:

Supporting details/examples/visuals:

Step 4:

Supporting details/examples/visuals:

Step 5:

Supporting details/examples/visuals:

(You can add additional steps if needed)

Conclusion

What should your audience have learned from you and why is it important?

Review the main points/steps:

Closing statement:

This graphic organizer can be printed from https://www.thegiftedguy.com/public-speaking.

Making a connection

While the five-minute speech was all about showing emotion in your voice, this one adds another layer. A good public speaker not only delivers information; they make a connection with the audience. This connection allows the speaker to take the audience on the journey with them.

How do you know if a speaker has connected to the audience? You get cues from the audience such as the nodding of heads when a point is made, laughter when saying something funny, or the ultimate goal of any speaker: applause.

Here is an example of a TED Talk where the speaker, a young boy from Kenya, devised an ingenious way to prevent lions in the savannah from killing the livestock on his family's farm:

When showing this to students, point out he is very nervous at first because English is not his primary language, and his confidence in his words is not strong. But at around 2:15, he is talking about how he tried to frighten the lions using a scarecrow, and he says, "but lions are very clever". Not only does this result in

> **TED TALK**
>
> A TED Talk on making peace with the lions: *My Invention That Made Peace with Lions* by Richard Turere.

laughter from the audience, Richard uses this audience reaction to gain his own confidence, which he indicates with a smile. But he wants more connection. So at 2:55, he talks about how he learned about electronics by taking his mom's radio apart, and he quips, "and that day, she almost killed me." Again laughter. Now he has warmed to the audience, and they are in sync. When he gets to the end of his personal story about outsmarting the lions by saying, "but I was sleeping in my bed," this time he not only gets laughter, he gets applause. And the look on his face in getting this continues to power his confidence.

You can further analyze the speech with students in the closing as he describes what this invention has done for him in reaching his dream of becoming an aircraft engineer. He practically has the audience eating out of his hand as he shows a visual of himself taking his first plane ride to come to speak at the TED event. And when he finishes, the crowd immediately gets to its feet, applauding. Richard earns this standing ovation by making several connections to the audience. He built this connection, and the payoff is the standing ovation.

There are several ways you can make this connection. Some of these are:

- Personal story
- Using humor
- Effective visuals
- Showing emotion
- The power of the pause

If you would like to see all of these in action, watch Brene Brown's *The Power of Vulnerability*.

> **TED TALK**
>
> To see several examples of making connections to the audience, watch *The Power of Vulnerability* by Brené Brown.

This is another good talk to analyze with students. Explain to students that one of the most effective ways to make this connection is for them to be vulnerable with the audience and share not just their knowledge, but their feelings as well. Brown does an excellent job of doing this and being vulnerable while talking about being vulnerable. She makes the ultimate connection of practicing what she preaches.

I will talk about using humor in a later chapter, but none of these strategies can be forced. They need to extend naturally from a speech, but that doesn't mean they cannot be planned and purposeful.

Shining a light

Detail is really important when communicating in general. If you leave out a detail, the message is not going to be clear. For example, if someone is giving a person directions to go to a restaurant but doesn't include a turn, the person is going to get lost. If a student is explaining a point in an essay and she doesn't provide a concrete example, the reader might not know what she is trying to say. Even if a person does something as simple as making a grocery list but leaves an item off, that item most likely is not going to be bought. Details matter.

This is especially true when teaching someone how to do something. The lack of details causes confusion, and that is never a good headspace for someone to be in when trying to learn. This is why I like to have students give the demonstrative speech because it forces them to pay attention to these details, a good habit to get into.

Here is a bonus TED Talk on how people learn and how students can use this when creating their demonstrative speeches:

> **TODD TALK**
>
> Here are several examples of why details matter that can be shown to students:
> https://youtu.be/8SsELDnPLql
>
>

> **TED TALK**
>
> A TED Talk on the neuroscience of learning: *The Neuroscience of Learning* by Siddharth Warrier.

8

Persuasive – the 15-minute speech

One of the benefits of learning to speak well for students is being able to get their way more often. This doesn't just happen when asking for something; one has to be convincing. Confidence has a way of being convincing, but there are other factors at play here as well. This is why the next speech I use with students is the 15-minute persuasive speech.

There is a difference between a speech meant to inform or teach, and one that is trying to persuade. Here is a good video on the difference between them: *Informative vs Persuasive by Communication Coach Alexander Lyon* https://www.youtube.com/watch?v=85gg_pgij4I.

Some expectations for this persuasive speech remain the same as the others. Speakers should still:

- Focus on the throughline
- Have emotion in their voice and not sound like a robot
- Be sure to make eye contact with the audience

New requirements being added are:

- Purpose must be to persuade an audience with an argument

DOI: 10.4324/9781003385981-9

- Must be 15 minutes in length
- Need to balance logos, ethos, and pathos effectively
- No visuals allowed (this is optional but I find this forces students to put the argument in their words)

Making a case

Arguing is an interesting thing. Like driving, everyone thinks they are good at it. But like most drivers out there, they are not as good as they think they are. People hear the phrase "making an argument" and think this means they have to be good at arguing. Even worse, the examples our politicians are setting for us are to bicker about petty things and try to be the loudest. This is not making an argument.

Making an argument should be looked at more as the role of a lawyer. Similar to a lawyer with his jury, the speaker is trying to convince and persuade an audience In order to do this, a lawyer has to make a case. The case involves presenting evidence that proves the client did not do it, bringing in reputable people to vouch for him or the evidence, and many times appealing to the emotional as well as the logical aspects of the argument. Although it seems contrary to what is represented in television and film, the lawyer is not ranting and raving in the courtroom. A lawyer, above all else, should be professional in the way the argument is handled. The same goes for students as they begin their persuasive argument.

In order to make a case, one has to answer the simple question of what, so what? In other words, the speaker makes a statement. That is the what. But in order to make a case, this has to be backed up with a reason, which might include a story, statistics, research, or other pieces of evidence. For example, I made the statement before that dogs are better pets than cats. Just because I said it doesn't make it so. It has got to have a so what. This is where the case is made. I could follow it up by saying several different so whats:

- ... because they are more affectionate than cats
- ... because you can take a dog for a walk, but not cats. Dog owners walk an average of 2,760 more steps a day
- ... because dogs can protect you from an intruder
- ... because according to the American Heart Association, owning a dog increases one's lifespan
- ... because dogs are used as therapy animals; have you ever seen a therapy cat?
- ... because dogs can be better trained than cats. They can actually be of use to sniff out drugs in suitcases at airports
- ... because according to Harvard Health, having a dog can lower your blood pressure
- ... because dogs come in all shapes and sizes to suit your needs. Cats come in one

These "so whats" are where the case is made. Once this is established, the speaker has an argument to make. This involves providing more detail and bringing in further evidence to strengthen the case, but this gives a clear purpose to the argument. Usually more than one "so what" is necessary for an argument in order to convince people. This is why there are three supporting paragraphs in an academic essay or three sections to a speech. Each one becomes its own "so what".

PRACTICE OPPORTUNITY

Have students give a speech about an argument that has no clear answer. Some of these might be:

- Kids their age should be allowed to vote.
- Which is better for the environment, paper or plastic?
- The death penalty should be abolished.
- Are violent video games bad for children?
- Homework should be banned.
- Are kids too addicted to their cell phones?
- Social media has improved communication.

> - Is human cloning a good thing?
> - Alternative energies can replace fossil fuels.
>
> They can flip a coin to see which side of the argument they are going to present.
> Make sure they are including the what, so what.

When showing this to students, point out how he uses all sorts of evidence such as:

> **TED TALK**
>
> *The Hidden Power of Smiling* by Ron Gutman is a TED Talk that makes a very clear case for the power of smiling using several pieces of evidence.

- Referring to studies such as the yearbook photos and the baseball cards
- Photos of babies smiling in the womb
- Smiles in natives cut off from civilization
- Experiments such as when people were asked to hold a pencil in their mouths
- Stories such as how Darwin felt about smiles
- Science, such as the stimulation of the brain and the effect on hormones

These all build his case. If your students don't believe this, at the end of the video, ask them if they themselves are not smiling. If they are, case closed.

Logos, pathos, and ethos

In order to make a good argument, a speech should use a mix of logos, pathos, and ethos. Figure 8.1 is an infographic that can sum these terms up for students fairly well.

114 ◆ Letting Student Voices Shine

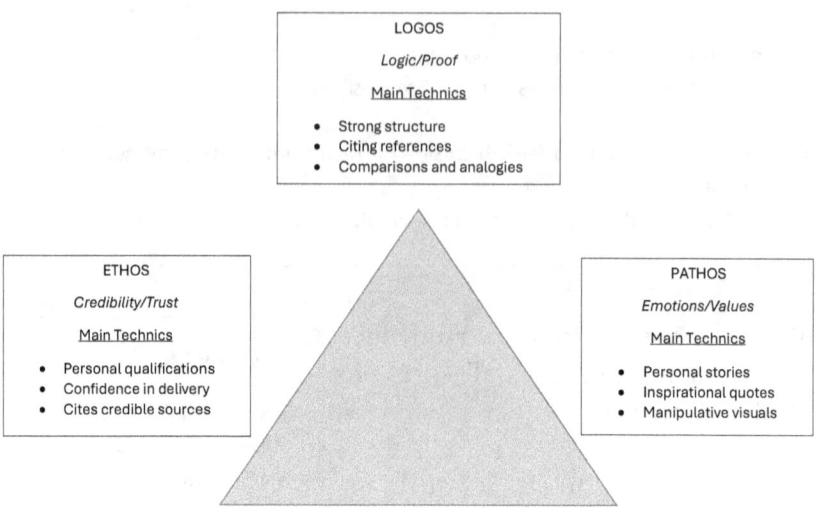

FIGURE 8.1

There are three ways for a speaker to gain the favor of an audience: appeal to the heart, the head, and/or the soul.

The head is the most obvious one. We try to persuade people all the time with our words and, in doing so, appeal to one's logic. Don't touch that stove, or you will burn yourself. If you eat too much sugar, you are going to get cavities. If you exercise, you will be healthier and live longer. We do this with evidence, comparisons, and facts. The tipping point of persuasion in logos is when someone thinks, "that makes sense".

The heart is another important way to persuade, some would say the thing that sets humans apart from AI. We make decisions with our hearts almost as much, if not more than with our heads. With the heart, a speaker is trying to get the audience to have sympathy or empathy for the argument. This is usually done with stories, personal anecdotes, and visuals. Because of this, the tipping point becomes that they feel for the argument.

The soul involves belief. Belief that the speaker is someone who should be listened to. Belief that your perspective or expertise is to be valued. And belief this person talking is a competent or reputable person. Speakers have to establish themselves as someone who should be listened to. The tipping point is that the audience trusts them. Because if the audience doesn't trust the speaker, then the argument will not be heard, no matter how much logic and emotion is put into it. An audience will rarely give the speaker this trust blindly. It must be earned.

Any one of these is powerful in itself, but think about how much more powerful it would be if a speaker were able to use all three of these. This is what you need to teach your students: how to use logos, pathos, and ethos together to persuade an audience.

This speaker establishes his ethos with his experience as an attorney. He uses lots of shocking statistics and comparisons as evidence of his logos. And he tells personal stories that make you feel the importance of his argument, thus appealing to pathos.

> **TODD TALK**
>
> To watch a video explaining what pathos, ethos, and logos are and how they work together, that can be shown to students go to:
>
> https://www.youtube.com/watch?v=M4-zum2mkP0
>
>

Logos – making sense of it

Logic was used by the ancient Greeks in the form of a syllogism. A syllogism had two statements which led to a conclusion. It looked like this:

> Johnny is tall
> It would take a tall person to reach the book on that shelf
> Johnny can reach the book on that shelf

> **TED TALK**
>
> *We Need to Talk About an Injustice by Bryan Stevenson* is a TED Talk that makes good use of all three: logos, pathos, and ethos.

Put the two pieces of information together to be able to make a logical conclusion. Now are we for certain Johnny can reach the book? Not 100%. But the logic makes sense that he should be able to. A logical conclusion has been made.

A person can use this logic to make an argument. An argument might look like this:

> Everyone in Johnny's family smokes
> People who smoke are more likely to get lung cancer
> Someone in Johnny's family is bound to get lung cancer

Again, there's no guarantee this will happen. But the chances are better. So good, in fact that someone listening to this logic will most likely be convinced of it.

To help students understand the idea of logic, you can have them construct their own syllogisms. It uses the simple formula of:

> If _____
> And _____
> Then _____

Have them work with a partner to check that the logic makes sense and that the connections lead into one another.

When teaching logos to students, how you present it to them is that a great way to make your argument stronger is to support it with evidence. Evidence is key to appealing to the head because it helps people see the logic.

Much like a lawyer, evidence can come in different forms. Some of these might be:

- Facts
- Studies
- Quotes/Statement from experts
- Hypotheticals
- Data/Statistics

The evidence should 1) be from a reputable source, 2) involve data that adds up, and/or 3) seem like it makes sense. This might involve having to conduct some research when writing their speech.

Here is an example of the difference between evidence and evidence from a reputable source:

> There are nearly half a million deaths in the United States every year due to smoking.

> The Center for Disease Control reports that 480,000 people die from smoking each and every year.

The Center for Disease Control is a well-known organization. Indicating the research came from there gives the evidence legitimacy; it adds to its ethos. Although the first statement gives information, that information is unfounded and could have been made up for all the audience knows. If the speaker is not a recognized expert on smoking or a doctor, why would the audience believe what is being said? By mentioning the source, the argument is strengthened.

In the introduction, the speaker mentions a study where folks are presented with two scenarios. In one, people are offered a 24-piece dinnerware set with eight dinner plates, eight bowls, and eight dessert plates. How much would they be willing to pay? The average came out to 390 pounds or nearly $500. In the second offering, it is a 40 piece set, also with eight dinner plates, eight bowls, and eight dessert plates, plus six cups and one saucer. The downside is there are also two broken cups and seven broken saucers. Here, people on average were willing to pay 192 pounds or $250. This makes no sense, though. Why pay more for less? Because the pathos, or heart plays tricks on people. They see the broken dinnerware and think the set has less value when logically it has more.

> **TED TALK**
>
> *The Counterintuitive Way to be More Persuasive by Niro Sivanathan* is a TED Talk that uses logos very well.

This evidence needs to above all fit into your case. But students need to understand that it is not enough to simply give the evidence. Someone using good logos needs to explain how it fits into a particular argument. This requires that the argument be clear and that the evidence supporting that argument is equally clear. Logic is lost when people cannot see how the two fit together.

Pathos – making a plea to the heart

When teaching pathos to your students, use this argument: statistics involving large numbers can be very powerful, but a single person's story can be much stronger. Say to them:

> 12.8 million people are starving in Africa.

They might think that is terrible. But would they really care? They might think this is awful, but they probably won't feel like they should do anything about it. It is only a number. It has no face. However, if you were to show them this image:

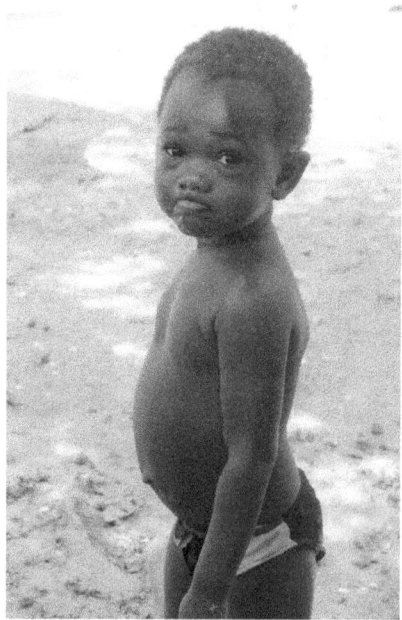

FIGURE 8.2

All of a sudden, this logical and unfeeling statistic has a face. It compels someone viewing it to care for this particular child and want to do something to help him. They will care for this child unlike they cared for the 12.8 million others they were told about before.

This is often how charities get people to donate to their causes. They don't give folks a bunch of numbers. Instead, the ASPCA shows cute dogs locked in cages, the Shriners have ill children make a plea for support, and the Red Cross shows the devastation of a hurricane or earthquake they are asking support for. Students can check out any of these websites and other such organizations to see how they appeal to pathos. Essentially they manipulate emotions. They make someone viewing it feel something, and that feeling makes someone want to agree with their side. This is pathos.

In analyzing this talk with students, point out how she uses personal stories to make the audience feel what it is like to be a girl from Nigeria and how her experiences make her argument about the danger of a single story.

> **TED TALK**
>
> *The Danger of a Single Story by Chimamanda Ngozi Adichie* is a TED Talk that uses pathos very well.

The best way for a speaker to convince an audience using pathos is the use of a personal story. These are often used in TED Talks and with good reason. These typically persuade because after they are told, people care more about what the person is talking about.

For example, let us say I want to convince you that wearing your seat belt is important for safety. I do so by telling you about the time I was in a car accident with a friend. I wore my seat belt and sustained minor injuries. My friend was not wearing his, was thrown from the car, and is now paralyzed from the waist down. This story of terrible tragedy would make you think twice about not wearing your seat belt. And it has appealed to your heart, not your head.

> **TED TALK**
>
> *I Survived a Terrorist Attack. Here's What I Learned by Gill Hicks* is a TED Talk that uses a personal story to elicit sympathy for her argument.

These stories can be stickier than mere statistics or facts. They stay with the audience a bit more, and they are more likely to remember them.

The other thing a personal story should do is show why the speaker cares about the argument. After all, if the person giving the speech doesn't seem to care about it, why should the audience? If someone is giving a speech about global warming, facts, studies, statistics, and hypotheticals should be provided to establish the logos. But an audience is ultimately wondering why this person cares about it. This is what Al Gore does in his TED Talk.

> **TED TALK**
>
> Al Gore uses a personal story to elicit sympathy for his scientific argument in *The Case for Optimism on Climate Change*.

Lots of compelling science and research are in this talk, but the part that gets me to care about it is the story he tells at the very end, 19 minutes into his speech. This is where the true persuasion takes place, and it also makes for a wonderful conclusion to his speech.

Ethos – having a reliable voice

The final one you need to teach your students is ethos. They have to create trust with the audience if these people are going to go on a journey with them. This can be established in many different ways. It could be credentials such as a degree or experience that makes you the expert to be talking about this topic. Because students may not have either of these, very often though it comes down to two things: their professionalism and confidence.

Have a conversation with your students about professionalism. A big part of being a good public speaker is being prepared. This is the ultimate act of professionalism, not that the speaker dresses in a suit. In fact, the organizers of TED have a no-tie rule. They don't want people trying to look too professional. They want people to be professional. The way a speaker shows this best is by having a well-rehearsed speech with technology that works. Although not perfect, mistakes have been minimized, and those that can be avoided have been.

The preparedness then leads to confidence. The more prepared someone is, the better their chances of being confident in what is being said. This is because there is a familiarity with it and knowing the evidence well enough to be able to communicate this clearly to the audience. A confident person sounds like she believes in what she is saying, so others believe her as well.

Bringing expertise to a speech makes it more credible. If someone is talking about the impact karate can have on one's discipline and mentions having taken part in it for over ten years, people are probably going to probably think this person knows something about it. A speaker could have a certain experience that makes him an expert. If he is talking about the joy Disney World can bring and he mentions he has been there five times this year alone, people will most likely think he has something to offer, definitely more than someone giving the same speech who has only been to Disney World once.

If a speaker claims to be knowledgeable about something yet lacks the expertise or experience, the audience will begin to question the ethos. For example, if a person is giving a speech about travel in France but tells the audience he has never visited there, what sort of insight will he be able to offer? Why would they believe him? This is why students should choose something they know about, to be able to bring their own experiences to the talk.

The expertise doesn't always need to come from the person doing the speaking, however. A speaker can cite experts to make a point, and the credibility of those sources allows the audience to trust what is being said. But if a student were to say, "I asked a couple of people about this" or "my neighbor down the street said this is so", then the audience is most likely not going to put much merit in what is being said. However, if the speaker says instead, "According to a study done at Harvard University" or "Albert Einstein once said", then the audience can believe these experts. It also shows that the presenter has the competence to find these sources in order to make an argument, which again shows professionalism.

> **TED TALK**
>
> *There's More to Life Than Being Happy* by Emily Esfahani Smith is a TED Talk that uses ethos very well.

In discussing this with students, note that the speaker is looking at something very pathos, which is happiness, but has to convince the audience that she has expertise in this topic, so she has to prove her ethos. She starts with a personal story and citing some research, but then she talks about how she spent five years interviewing people and studying research by psychologists, neuroscientists, and philosophy. When someone studies something for five years, that gives them a certain amount of ethos that others do not possess.

Ultimately your students will need to convince the audience, "Why should I listen to this person? What makes them the one to deliver this speech?" If the audience doesn't believe them in their soul, if they do not seem reliable, and/or if they lack the professionalism to allow trust in what is being said, persuading them will be next to impossible.

Finding the balance

When using logos, ethos, and pathos, students do not have to use them equally. A speech about putting a colony on Mars is going to need a lot of logos in order to convince others. One about a particular skill, such as how to cook something, might need more ethos to satisfy people that the speaker knows their way around a kitchen. If a speaker wants to get people motivated to do something, pathos is definitely going to move people a lot more than information will. The speaker has to determine which of these methods of persuasion will best meet the purpose of the speech. The triangle is not going to be equal in its angles; it is going to be oblong.

For example, in an expository speech a student might have to deliver facts that appeal to the audience's logic as well as being a reliable voice, but there is not much reason to have to sway their heart:

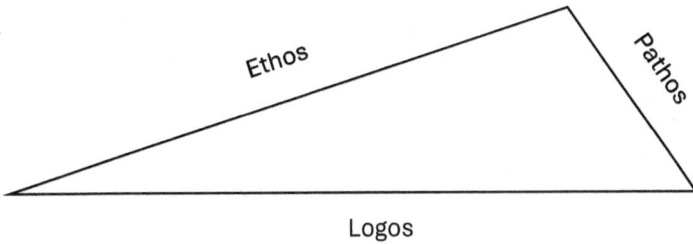

FIGURE 8.3

An inspirational speech, on the other hand, will use much more pathos and ethos, but maybe only a little logos:

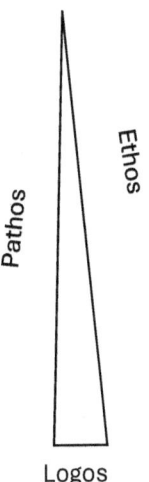

FIGURE 8.4

A persuasive speech usually needs to use all three of these strategies in some form so it will look more balanced than most. There might be small adjustments to which one is focused on more depending on which is argued the strongest. In this scenario the speaker is trying to persuade the audience to read the book *Ender's Game*:

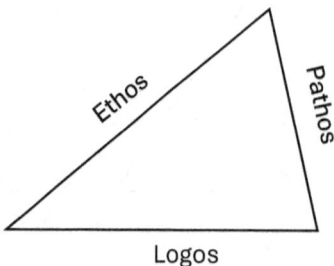

FIGURE 8.5

In this case, the pathos is not going to be as convincing as the logos or ethos, but it is still present.

The counterargument

One of the more effective ways a speaker can persuade an audience is to anticipate their objections about the argument and address them. The reason why it is so effective is that the speaker is essentially cutting off any argument the audience might naturally be forming in their heads.

For example, going back to the dogs-being-better-than-cats argument. Someone might be thinking, as the speaker is espousing the many benefits of dogs, "Just what are the benefits of a cat over a dog?" If the speaker can mention these and then counterargue, this audience member is not going to doubt the argument. The counterargument might sound like this:

> **TODD TALK**
>
> To watch a video explaining the benefit of a counterargument that can be shown to students, go to: https://youtu.be/1dLZM4DDQwc
>
>

Some might argue that cats are better than dogs because they are low maintenance and do not need to be taken outside to use the restroom. But you do need to buy and maintain the kitty litter box which can be a lot of work and puts the smell inside your house rather than outside where you don't have to deal with it.

A good counterargument can take the wind out of any doubts the audience might be forming. Besides that, it strengthens the argument of the speaker because it exposes the weaknesses in the case and then shores it up by making a counterpoint.

> **ACTIVITY**
>
> Have students take the argument they are going to make in their 15-minute speech and try and brainstorm five possible arguments someone might have against it.
>   If they are having trouble coming up with some, have them move around the room and ask others what sorts of arguments they can think of against them. Have them collect these arguments and then come up with ways to counter them.
>   These can then be the basis for the counterarguments they present in their speech.

Finding the proper counterargument takes a bit of anticipation. A person has to figure out logically what are the arguments that can be made against their position. It involves taking on other perspectives. Take for instance the argument that smoking should be banned. There are a lot of good arguments that can be made for this point. But as much as it pains you, you have to try and see other people's points of view. Some people might see it differently:

- Smoker
- Civil rights lawyer
- Government
- Law enforcement
- Someone who works for the tobacco industry
- Store than sells cigarettes

Their possible counterarguments could be:

- Allows some people to reduce their stress (smoker)
- Takes away choice from people, civil liberties (civil rights lawyer)
- Brings in money from the taxes (government)
- Making it illegal will simply create black markets (law enforcement)
- Will cost of lot of jobs for people in the smoking industry (someone who works for the tobacco industry)
- Will take money away from people (store that sells cigarettes)

Any one of these could be a counterargument. A speaker cannot address them all, though. So one has to try and guess which one or two would resonate most with an audience. No one likes to have their civil liberties messed with, so this could be the counterargument to attack. It might look like this:

> Some can argue that banning smoking is taking away the right for people to choose. That this is a violation of their civil liberties because they can make the decision to harm themselves by smoking for themselves, it is their right. Of course, the problem with this is that they are not the only ones who are hurt by their decision. Second-hand smoke kills approximately 41,000 people a year. These people didn't have a choice. You could argue people could smoke in the privacy of their own homes and not affect others, but they might have spouses or children living with them who are not getting to make that choice for themselves.

> **TED TALK**
>
> This TED Talk discusses the importance of listening to those you do not agree with: *Why It's Worth Listening to People you Disagree With* by Zachary R. Wood.

This speaker has flipped the script and used the counterargument of personal choice to strengthen their case. That personal choice affects the personal choice of others all of a sudden diminishes the argument for having it.

Here is a TED Talk you can show students that explains the importance of listening to the other side:

Practice opportunity

Have students determine the possible counterarguments for these arguments:

- Democracy is the best form of government
- Nuclear weapons should be banned
- Final exams should be abolished
- Year-round school is better for students
- Math is the most important school subject
- In-person school is better than online
- Animals should not be kept in zoos
- We should be spending money to explore space
- Gum chewing should be permitted in school
- AI is good for humanity

> **TED TALK**
>
> *Why School Should Start Later for Teens* by Wendy Troxel
>
> This TED Talk not only makes valid arguments but also brings up the most likely counterarguments and shows the flaws in them.

Then have them determine how to counter the counterargument.

The persuasive speech

Outline for persuasive speech
(approximately 2,000 words in length)

My topic:

Introduction

Opening Statement/Hook

Throughline:

Body

Main Point 1:

Supporting details/examples:

Possible counterarguments:

Main Point 2:

Supporting details/examples:

Possible counterarguments:

Main Point 3:

Supporting details/examples:

Possible counterarguments:

Conclusion

What does this look like if you get what you are asking for?

Review the main arguments:

Closing statement

For a copy of this graphic organizer go to https://www.thegifted-guy.com/public-speaking.

15-Minute Persuasive Speech

Student: _____ Topic: _____

Overall	Content	Presentation	Persuasion
Excellent	• Presenter has a good/full understanding of the argument and can make it clear to the audience why they feel this way. • The content has a clear throughline that the audience can follow. • The speech uses lots of details and examples to support the argument.	• Presenter has a good pace/tone that can easily be understood. • Presents the speech rather than reads it, making it more like a conversation. • Contains a personal story that connects speaker to the audience. • Speech should be 14:00 to 16:00 minutes in length.	• Presenter uses either statistics or data to help the audience to see their side, making a clear connection to the argument. • Presenter has appropriate body language that shows the passion they have for the topic. • Presents shows not just their side but the other side as well, making counter arguments.
Good	• Presenter has a general understanding of the argument but does not make a strong argument why they feel this way. • The content has a throughline that the audience can follow most of the time but occasionally gets off-topic. • The speech uses details and examples to support this argument but is not consistent with it.	• Presenter has a good pace/tone that can easily be understood but every once in a while • Presents the speech most of the time, but occasionally reads it. • Contains a personal story but does not connect the speaker to the audience. • Speech ends one minute before or after the time range.	• Presenter uses either statistics or data to help the audience to see their side, but does not make a clear connection to their argument. • Presenter uses body language but it does not necessarily convey the passion they have for the topic. • Presents shows both sides but does not necessarily make the counter arguments.
Needs Improvement	• Presenter has a limited understanding of the argument and cannot make it clear to the audience why they feel this way. • The content lacks a clear throughline, making it very difficult to follow. • The speech lacks details and examples to support this argument.	• Presenter has a pace/tone that makes it difficult to understood at times. • Often reads the speech rather than presenting it, making it sound robotic. • Does not contain a personal story • Speech ends less or more than two minutes of the time range.	• Presenter does not use either statistics or data to help the audience to see their side. • Presenter uses little to no body language, or body language that shows disinterest. • Presents shows only one side of the argument.

FIGURE 8.6

Shining a light

A persuasive argument can be one of the most beneficial for students to learn because if they master it, they get their way a lot more. The key is finding the right balance of pathos, ethos, and logos. Which one is going to be the one that tips the scales? Which one is going to cause people to say to themselves, "They have a really good point?" There is no one way to give a persuasive speech. The effectiveness comes in determining which balance is going to persuade people the most and how to accomplish this.

Figure 8.6 is a rubric you can use for the 15-minute persuasive speech.

This rubric can be printed from https://www.thegiftedguy.com/public-speaking.

9

Oratorical – the 20-minute TED Talk

You have been building up the speaking endurance of your students over time, starting with the five-minute speech and leading up to the final performance: the 20-minute speech. Like a runner adding more miles to her regimen, this 20-minute speech should feel achievable now to your students.

Carrying forward from other speeches, some of the requirements that should remain for them are:

- Focus on the throughline
- Have emotion in their voice and not sound like a robot
- Be sure to make eye contact with the audience
- If using visuals, make sure they are meaningful
- The use of a personal story

There are some new requirements being added, such as:

- Purpose must be to inspire
- Must be 20 minutes in length
- Need to have a well-developed and purposeful introduction and conclusion
- Have hooks throughout the speech
- Use of non-verbals

DOI: 10.4324/9781003385981-10

Figure 9.1 shows what the requirements would look like in the form of a rubric.

This rubric can be printed from https://www.thegiftedguy.com/public-speaking.

The challenge of a speech of this length for students, or anyone for that matter, is maintaining the attention of an audience over this extended period of time. Sure, the human mind is designed to be able to listen for 20 minutes, but if the speaker doesn't get the attention of the audience at first or if the focus starts to wane, those listening won't be around long enough to get the message.

A speaker has to figure out ways to not only get the audience to listen at first but to keep listening. The best way to do this is to have strategic hooks placed throughout the speech.

Hooks

A hook is just something interesting that causes the audience to reengage with the speech. There are several things a speaker can use as a hook, but five to consider would be:

- Story
- Video/graphic
- Rhetorical question
- Provocative statement
- Humor – this will be talked about in the next chapter

> **YOUTUBE**
>
> *Great TED Talk Hooks by Jancey Clark* is a video you can show to students to introduce hooks to them and shows them being used in TED Talks.

Stories

Stories are one of the easiest hooks for students to use, and it does a few things. 1) A story is usually very interesting, and people

20-Minute Oratorical Speech Rubric

Student: _____ Topic: _____

Overall	Engagement	Structure	Presentation
Excellent	<ul><li>There is a clear and interesting throughline in the speech with a consistent thesis keeping us focused on the idea wanting to be spread.</li><li>The speaker connects in a meaningful way with the audience by sharing a personal story or experience which links to the topic.</li><li>The speech is inspiring to the audience while the speaker is also passionate and knowledgeable about the topic.</li></ul>	<ul><li>Hooks are used throughout the speech consistently to keep the attention of the audience.</li><li>The introduction is well developed and it sets the groundwork for the rest of the speech.</li><li>The closing is well developed and it ends the speech effectively.</li><li>The speech is between 18 and 22 minutes.</li></ul>	<ul><li>Speaker's voice is consistently clear and understandable, and has a controlled pace that is appropriate to whatever is being talked about.</li><li>Speaker presents the entire speech, making consistent eye contact throughout, does not read speech.</li><li>Speaker uses body language that conveys the appropriate feeling of the speech.</li></ul>
Good	<ul><li>There is a throughline in the speech with a thesis, but not always consistently mentioned causing audience to lose focus of the idea being spread.</li><li>The speaker shares a personal story or experience which links to the topic but does not connect with its meaning.</li><li>The speech is inspiring to the audience but the speaker doesn't show enough passion and knowledge about the topic.</li></ul>	<ul><li>Hooks are used throughout the speech but not consistently or they do not connect to the throughline.</li><li>An introduction is used but it does not set up the rest of the speech very well.</li><li>A closing is used but does not end as effectively as it could.</li><li>The speech is less than 18 minutes or more than 22 by just a minute or two.</li></ul>	<ul><li>Speaker's voice is clear and understandable for the most part, although either occasionally mutters or the pace is not consistently appropriate to whatever is being talked about.</li><li>Speaker presents the speech most of the time, making eye contact, but there are times when it is read and the speaker is looking down.</li><li>Speaker most times shows body language that conveys the appropriate feeling of the speech.</li></ul>
Needs Improvement	<ul><li>There is not a clear and/or interesting throughline in the speech, causing it to jump around and lack focus, making the audience unsure of the idea trying to be spread.</li><li>The speaker does not share a personal story or experience or it does not links to the topic.</li><li>The speech lacks inspiration or is delivered without much passion and knowledge about the topic.</li></ul>	<ul><li>Hooks are not used or used seldomly throughout the speech.</li><li>An introduction is barely used or is not used, failing to set up the rest of the speech.</li><li>A closing is barely used or is not used, causing the ending to just peter out.</li><li>The speech is less than 18 minutes or more than 22 by several minutes.</li></ul>	<ul><li>Speaker's voice is not clear and/or understandable, either muttering often or not having a controlled pace that is appropriate to whatever is being talked about.</li><li>Speaker reads the speech most of the time, looking down a lot and not making eye contact.</li><li>Speaker doesn't use much body language to convey the appropriate feeling of the speech.</li></ul>

FIGURE 9.1

love to hear them, so it will refocus an audience that has been sitting and getting a lot of information. 2) It illustrates points by bringing them to life. A speaker can talk about statistics concerning the benefits of getting a colonoscopy, but sharing a story about someone who should have gotten one and didn't, and then ended up dying will make it real. 3) It connects the speaker to their audience because telling a story is more personal and makes the speech more of a conversation than a formal lecture.

There will be more about telling personal stories in the next chapter on igniting your passion.

Video/graphic

I do not give a speech without a slidedeck. I do this for reasons I have talked about already, but one of the advantages is that a well-chosen visual or using a video with someone else's voice can re-hook an audience. I can tell an audience all about my experiences as a teacher in education and share my expertise, but sometimes hearing it from another perspective can be more effective.

Once I was leading an all-day professional development session about working with twice-exceptional or 2e children. I spent hours giving teachers data, studies, and experiences. I threw in a couple of clips of students sharing their own experiences, mostly just to give my voice a rest and allow another to be heard. Overwhelmingly this is what the audience of over 200 reported as being the most memorable thing in their post-PD survey. Something I had included as a throwaway ended up having the greatest impact on my audience. So I began to do this more often with my presentations, getting a similar reaction.

> **TED TALK**
>
> *The Paradox of Choice by Barry Schwartz* is a TED Talk that uses comic strips throughout to summarize and make points. They act as great hooks.
>
> ⚠ I would not show the entire thing to students as, about 11:40 into the talk, he shows a comic strip that is intended for adults.

A well-placed visual can act as a hook. One that I have seen used often is a cartoon strip that relates to what you are talking about:

Rhetorical question

According to Andrew Dlugan in his article "How to Use Rhetorical Questions in Your Speech", there are nine different ways to use a rhetorical question. They are:

1. Engage the audience to think
2. Invite your audience to agree with you
3. Stir emotions
4. Emphasize a previous statement
5. Invoke misdirection
6. Ask and answer a question your audience might be thinking
7. Answer a question with a rhetorical one
8. Ask a series of questions to give the audience many possibilities
9. Ask a series of questions that lead to the answer you want (Dlugan, 2012)

Probably the most effective one is the first one, getting an audience to think. A rhetorical question almost always engages the audience and re-hooks them into a talk. Audiences typically come to a speech curious. Otherwise why would they even be there? But a speaker can make them even more curious by asking the right question.

A rhetorical question is a question meant to provoke thought. Some examples of rhetorical questions would be:

- Who wouldn't want to be a millionaire?
- Why should people care about the environment?
- How would you react if someone said you couldn't live your dreams?
- Where would you go if space travel were possible?
- What would you do if you were in that situation?

- When do you think we need to do something about gas-powered cars?

These sorts of questions can be asked by your students at the beginning of their speech, throughout the middle, and in their conclusion. However, they should be strategically placed and have something to do with their throughline.

> **ACTIVITY**
>
> Have students watch the following video on six tips for being more effective at rhetorical questions: *Rhetorical Questions for Public Speaking by Communication Coach Alexander Lyon.*
> https://www.youtube.com/watch?v=XIh2obdPpOU. Then have them think of three rhetorical questions they could use in their speech in order to spark curiosity. To make it easier, have them think of one at the beginning of the speech, during the middle, and for the conclusion.

Provocative statement

A provocative statement as a hook is almost the opposite of a rhetorical question. Unlike a rhetorical question which doesn't necessarily have an answer, a provocative statement begs for one. An answer the audience will be sitting on the edge of their seats waiting for the speaker to reveal. This makes the audience much more likely to listen to the speech, which is why it is such an effective hook.

The title to Shonda Rhimes' TED Talk is *My Year of saying Yes to Everything*.

She declares to the audience that for an entire year she pledged to say yes to anything that scared her or took her out of her comfort zone. These are the first words she says in the speech. Of course, the audience

> **TED TALK**
>
> *My Year of Saying Yes to Everything by Shonda Rhimes* is a TED Talk where its provocative statement makes you want to listen to more.

wants to know what happened with this. This makes them curious about just how far she was willing to go with this mantra. Surely there are interesting stories she will tell to go along with this. It hooks the audience. They wonder what their own life would be like if they, too, did this.

A provocative statement can come from someone who is challenging the very world they exist in. When Cameron Russell claims, "looks aren't everything, believe me, I'm a model", it gets one thinking; This must be pretty important if she is challenging the very world in which she makes her living.

> **TED TALK**
>
> *Looks Aren't Everything. Believe Me, I'm a Model.* Cameron Russell is a TED Talk where the speaker challenges her own status quo.

So how do you teach students to include provocative statements as hooks in their speeches? Provocative statements don't always sit so well in an educational setting, and you don't want to get parents upset because a student said something a bit too provocative for the classroom. But a provocative statement doesn't need to be controversial; it is merely a statement people weren't expecting. It is a contrarian statement. If one is expecting the conversation to go right, it is taking it left.

Here is a provocative statement that we couldn't have imagined would have come true 20 years ago. "What if we could make food that tastes and looks like meat but is totally made out of plants?" It is about provoking thought, not controversy.

> **TED TALK**
>
> *The Art of Misdirection* by Apollo Robbins
> How does a pickpocket study human behavior? Bet you want to find out. That is what makes it provocative.

Here is an excellent TED Talk that begins with a provocative statement. The speaker talks about studying human behavior. You expect him to say he is a psychologist, or an anthropologist, or even someone who studies ethics. But what you don't expect is for him to declare that he is a pickpocket. It immediately provokes one's thinking as to what a pickpocket could have to offer about human behavior.

> **PRACTICE SPEECH**
>
> Have students take one of these contrarian statements and make a mini-speech about it.
>
> - More money doesn't make you happier
> - Improved technology has not improved communication
> - Going to college does not guarantee a good job
> - You learn more from failure than you do from success
> - The more people criticize it, the better the idea
> - Winning isn't everything
> - Most of what you learn in school, you will never use again
> - Nice guys often finish last
> - Your EQ is more important than your IQ
> - A bad plan is better than no plan

For their own speeches, students can look for opportunities where their thought process goes against the norm of what is expected. Those are the places where they can declare this to the audience and then back up this assertion with evidence and logic.

No matter which of these hooks students decide to use, they shouldn't happen by accident. They should be strategically placed and well thought out. As students are writing their speech, they should look for opportunities to use them in an organic manner. In other words, they should not be forcing these into the speech. A speaker might be constructing her speech and think, "This might be a good place for a story to illustrate this", or wonder whether a rhetorical question might make sense at this particular point. It shouldn't be, "I haven't had a hook for a while, so I am going to throw in a provocative statement here out of the blue". It needs to feel like part of the natural progression. Students simply need to look for spots where these might be used.

The graphic organizer at the end of this chapter has a place for students to consider the types of hooks that might best fit in each section of the speech. There doesn't need to be a hook in every section, but the longer the speech, the more a speaker will have to employ multiple hooks to maintain the focus of the audience.

> **FOR PRACTICE**
>
> Have students come up with possible hooks for the following topics:
> - Here is a book everyone should read
> - Renewable energy sources
> - What if this had happened in history instead of that?
> - Why raising kids can be a challenge
> - The human body
> - On-line learning is effective
> - It is important to learn to speak in public
> - Impressionistic art
> - Why should we learn about Ancient Greece?
> - AI is the wave of the future
>
> Ask students to come up with three different hooks for each topic. Then have them determine as a class which one is most effective.

Having a purposeful opening

In a five-minute or ten-minute speech, there isn't a whole lot of time to explain oneself before getting to the heart of the speech. If a person only has five minutes to speak, then a two-minute introduction is going to use up too much of the time. It is like a short story that has to establish its characters, setting, and conflict all within a couple of pages to leave enough pages to tell the rest of the story. But with a 20-minute speech, a speaker has time to develop an introduction and to build up to a climax much like a novelist would with a book. A novel spends its first few chapters developing the beginning of the book. It takes its time and sets the stage properly. But what does that look like in a speech?

What is the purpose of the opening of a speech?

> **TED TALK**
>
> *How to Spot a Liar* by Pamela Meyer is a TED Talk that has a very effective opening.

Pamela Myer not only opens with an excellent hook by declaring, "The person sitting to your right is a liar", to capture the attention of her audience, but she spends the first

7:44 of her 18:33 speech setting up the culture of liars and the truths behind this world before getting into the throughline of her speech, which is on liespotting.

Just like a story which is divided up into a beginning, middle, and end, each has a distinctive purpose. Typically the beginning of the speech has four main purposes. They are:

- Get the audience hooked
- Provide the context of what people need to know
- Establish the throughline
- Transition to the main part of the speech

During this time, you are also establishing the tone of the speech. If you are formal in your demeanor and use sobering statistics to establish a solemn tone, the audience knows they are in for a serious talk. If, on the other hand, you are more casual, use humor, and have some fun visuals, this talk might be more entertaining and light-hearted. There are genres in films and books. These have to stay fairly consistent in tone in order to establish the genre. Just like a novel, once the tone has been established in the speech, it needs to stay fairly consistent. Students don't want to tell an off-color joke in the middle of a talk on the effects of alcoholism, nor do they want to include a story of someone dying in their good-humored speech concerning the influences of *The Simpsons* on culture. Inconsistent shifts in tone can ruin a speech. There are some who can deftly move back and forth between tones in a speech, but it is only for the very skilled and has to be very planned out.

One TED Talk you can show to students that demonstrates a shift between various tones quite effectively is *The 3 A's of Awesome by Neil Pasricha*.

In my opinion, this is the best TED Talk I have seen. It combines stories with effective visuals. It changes back and forth in tone effortlessly, talking about serious things such as the breakup of his marriage and how bad things can

> **TED TALK**
>
> *The 3 A's of Awesome by Neil Pasricha* is a TED Talk that moves back and forth between tones seamlessly.

happen to you, with much humor, such as a football player who likes to do needlepoint, to poignant sections, such as remembering the little things that bring such joy and honoring his parents in the audience. Point out to your students how he does this in one single story where he tells the story of going on a trip with a friend and how they blocked the seals on the beach in a photo, getting the audience to laugh. Then, a minute later, he shares this very same friend committed suicide. And what makes him able to do this is a solid structure where he tells the audience exactly what he sets out to do and directs the audience clearly.

This really comes down to how the audience feels about the delivery of the speech. If the speaker doesn't establish a tone, the audience will establish one for themselves, which can cause chaos. If the audience is confused by the speaker's tone, they will more than likely be confused by the speech.

You need to stress to students that the beginning of the speech is so important because if not done well, the audience simply stops listening. They may have insightful and groundbreaking things to share later in their speech, but if the audience is confused, lost, or, worst of all, bored, none of this will be heard.

You can show your students how each of these purposes builds on one another in order to develop the speech:

- Get them hooked – there are several ways to do this. Some of these include:
  - Deliver a dose of drama
  - Ignite curiosity
  - Show a compelling photo/video
  - Tease
  - Audience involvement

Some of these have already been talked about at length in this chapter. The two I have not discussed are the tease and audience involvement.

Although it is important for students to be transparent and let their audience know what is going on at all times, it is also alright to tease them to get them more interested in what is being talked about.

Take, for example, this TED Talk on the magic of interactivity:

The speaker starts out with a good hook by telling a story about Mario Brothers and why it is so intriguing for people to play. This certainly engages and hooks the audience. But what is more of a hook is that immediately when he walks on the stage, he places a crumpled-up brown paper sack on a stool and makes no mention of it. The audience is left wondering, what the heck is that bag doing there and more importantly, what is in it? He doesn't even touch the bag for the first nine minutes of his speech, but it is just sitting there, teasing the audience the entire time.

> **TED TALK**
>
> *The Magic of Interactivity by Hayden Childress* is a TED Talk that uses a tease well.

Teasing an audience makes them curious to know more. This is why movie previews are known as teasers. They show just enough of the story but leave enough out that it makes one want to see the entire film. Students can apply this same concept to their speeches. They can introduce something that they are going to reveal later or show only a piece of the puzzle, leaving the audience to guess what the entire picture might be.

The second of these hooks is audience involvement. This makes an audience an active participant rather than a passive passenger. This can be as simple as asking for a show of hands in answer to a question, to actually bringing people on stage to demonstrate something. It could be asking them to check something about themselves, such as when Amy Cuddy asks the audience to look at the way they are sitting in her TED Talk on body language which will be discussed later in this chapter. When watching it, point out to students that audience members are suddenly so much more aware of themselves.

Just remind students that the hook at the beginning of the speech is the most important part because, without it, the audience will not come on this journey with the speaker. Students will have to get the audience interested enough to make them want to hear more.

♦ Provide the context of what people need to know

Once the audience is hooked, the speaker needs to give the background information required in order to understand what is going to be talked about. The speaker cannot just start talking about a book without giving its name, author, and basic plot. Or begin teaching a skill without establishing what the skill is.

Imagine a school teacher trying to teach students about a triangle. Depending on its context, this could refer to several different things. A triangle in math is a shape where you can determine its angles. A triangle in Language Arts could be a love triangle in a book such as *Pride and Prejudice* who is trying to decide between Mr. Darcy and George. In science, it could be a physical place where there are interesting weather patterns, such as the Bermuda Triangle. In music, the triangle is an instrument. In physical education, a triangle offense applies to basketball. Without the context, the audience doesn't know which direction the speaker is going in, and this can cause a lot of confusion.

Part of this context is speaking in the language of the audience. Does the audience know the world of the speaker, and if not, what must the speaker explain so that they can understand it? How much needs to be shared is a fine line. The difficulty sometimes is that when one already exists in that world, it can be challenging to remember what it was like when they did not. They have to go back to the mantra of "the audience is ignorant" and provide enough information for them not to be.

One way to check this is for students to run their speeches by their parents. It is often said that children and their parents speak a different language. If they give the speech to their parents and the parents understand it well, then context has probably been established. But if there is confusion, some additional context may need to be added in order to clear things up.

◆ Establish the throughline

The throughline is the heart of the speech. If a speaker gets through the opening and has not stated the throughline at least once in a single, memorable sentence, then what does the audience have to focus on? It helps to state this throughline more than once.

Have students ask themselves to sum up their own throughline in a single sentence. If they are unable to do this, they need to go back to the drawing board and make sure they can. Then insert this sentence in the introduction and in other places in the speech to remind the audience of what it is.

I have seen some speakers even put the throughline on a slide to show the audience, which almost guarantees that this message will be clear. Pranav Mistry, in his TED Talk on the potential of sixth sense technology, shared this slide with his audience within the first few minutes of his speech (Figure 9.2).

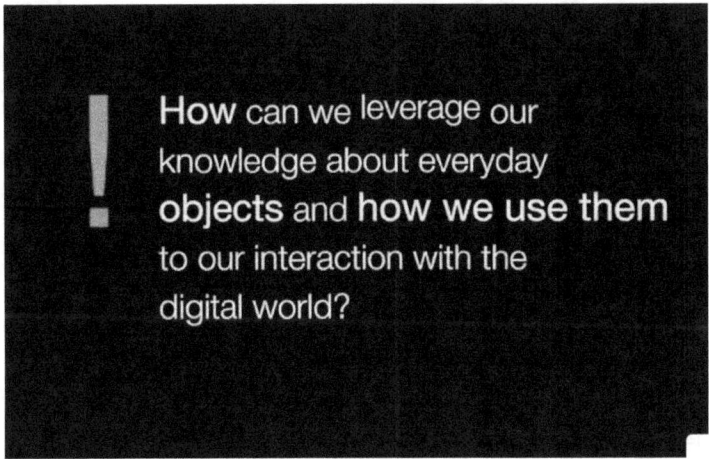

FIGURE 9.2

It is the throughline of his talk and his life's work. And given that his topic is a fairly complicated one, although one that he does a good job explaining the context very clearly, it certainly helps to state this throughline in such a way that there is no confusing what it is.

- Transition to the main part of the speech

As the tour guide of this speech, you have to make the audience aware when you are moving in another direction. This can be subtle, but then you risk that the audience will not get the cue and fail to follow. Remembering that the audience is ignorant, you should just come out and tell them where you are taking them next. No one is going to complain that you guided them too much, but it is easy for an audience to complain they were not led enough.

Once you have stated that throughline, transition by telling the audience what you intend to do with it. For example, you might say:

- There are three key points I'll be discussing …
- I want to begin by … and then I'll move on to …
- We'll be covering … from these points of view …
- So what does this have to do with my point? Here is the first reason …
- This presentation is divided into five parts …
- Now that you're aware of the overview, let's begin with…
- First, let's start with …
- I will first talk about …
- My first point covers …
- To get started, let's look at …

TODD TALK

To watch a video breaking down an opening that can be shown to students, go here:
https://youtu.be/ggbFRUaN2ro

All four of these elements should be present in the opening of a speech to make sure things are very clear. Can a student start a speech without a hook? Certainly, but it is usually not as interesting. Can a speaker give the context later in the speech? Sure, but by that time is the audience so confused that there is no recovering? Can someone skip the throughline? The answer to that is no. Following this structure ensures that the framework of communication is followed and, remember, that's what we want from students:

for them to communicate an idea in a way that the audience understands. But it does not guarantee this communication is clear. Students still need to provide the appropriate detail and clarity for this to happen. Laying this all out in the opening starts it off on the correct foot.

Having a purposeful closing

I always say, a great closing cannot help a poor speech, but a poor closing can ruin a great speech. Much like the introduction, the conclusion has a specific purpose. The three things for a closing would be:

- Restate the throughline
- Summarize main points
- Leave the audience with something to think about

In the conclusion she transitions by stating that she is going to leave the audience with three calls to action. They are:

> **TED TALK**
>
> *The Power of Introverts* by Susan Cain is a TED Talk with a very powerful closing.

1) Stop the madness for constant group work
2) Go to the wilderness
3) Take a good look at your own suitcase and why you put it there

It is a satisfying encapsulation because at the beginning of the speech, she walked out with a suitcase and talked about how she used to keep her books in there when she went to summer camp. What a great way to end the speech while also inspiring those who are introverts to share a little more about the things they keep in their suitcases.

The first two purposes of a conclusion are fairly simple. Just have students restate the throughline clearly and summarize briefly the main points of the speech, which is just a reiteration of the supporting points. There may need to be some coaching on how much information needs to be provided in the brief summary. Some students want to give just a bullet point. Others want to retell their entire middle part of the speech. What they need is somewhere in between. It should be a summary of what the point was and why it is important or relevant.

The question, though, is how do students leave the audience with something to think about? Tell them to imagine themselves as a lawyer giving their final argument. They have been building this case using a lot of evidence and stories. But this is the last thing they are going to say that the jurors are most likely to remember. The same thing goes for the audience of a speech. Does the speaker want to leave them with something to think about, or does the ending simply fizzle out? Which one is going to cause the audience to remember what the speech was about?

Of course, they will want to finish strong and with something of note. They could use several different strategies in order to accomplish this, such as:

- Call to action
- Personal commitment
- Values and vision
- Satisfying encapsulation
- Lyrical inspiration

TODD TALK

To watch a video breaking down a closing that can be shown to students, go here:
https://youtu.be/NWSmGqGseq4

However, they will want to make sure the very last words spoken are ones worth hearing. I have already used the Brene Brown TED Talk, *The Power of Vulnerability*, as an excellent example of a speech that makes connections with the audience. She continues this into her conclusion where she finishes with the following inspiring words,

And the last, which I think is probably the most important, is to believe that we're enough, because when we work from a place, I believe, which says "I'm enough", then we stop screaming and start listening, we're kinder and gentler to the people around us, and were kinder and gentler to ourselves.

However, after delivering this powerful message, which definitely gives you something to think about, she speaks these final four words, which nearly wreck its sentiment:

That's all I have.

Total buzzkill. And maybe it's just me, but her message gets muddled because those final words take me out of the moment. Students need to finish their speech on a high note, not as an afterthought.

> **TED TALK**
>
> Although a great speech, Brene Brown's final words in her TED *Talk The Power of Vulnerability* diminish the impact it has.

The oratorical speech

(2,500–3,000 words in length)

My topic:

Introduction

Opening Statement:

Opening Used:
- Deliver a dose of drama
- Ignite curiosity
- Show a compelling photo/video
- Tease
- Audience participation

How was it used?

Hooks:

Throughline:

Body

Main Point 1:

Supporting details/examples:

Hooks:

Main Point 2:

Supporting details/examples:

Hooks:

Main Point 3:

Supporting details/examples:

Hooks:

Conclusion

Restate the throughline with a transition:

Closing statement:

Which closing was used:
- Call to action
- Personal commitment
- Values and vision
- Satisfying encapsulation
- Lyrical inspiration

How was it used?

Inspirational message:

Shining a light

The longer the speech, the more the speaker has to do to keep the attention of the audience. A speaker recognizing he only has about ten minutes of the audience's attention, even with the right hook, has to reengage them throughout its length. Students can do this in several ways.

Because there is more time to speak, the speech needs to be better developed, not necessarily just by adding additional content. This development shows in the opening of the speech where the speaker must prepare the audience for what they are going to listen to. It finishes with the closing where the speaker sums up the wisdom or message of the talk and leaves the audience with something to remember.

Although not an exact science, a 20-minute speech should break down as per Figure 9.3 if it is well-developed.

FIGURE 9.3

10

The little things matter

When it comes to public speaking, students can do the big things such as having a solid structure, a clear throughline, and a strong voice. But the primary difference between a good and a great speaker are the little things. Little nuances such as effective transitions, using hands to add to the communication, injecting humor into the speech, and how much passion is shown while speaking.

Passion causes people to fall in love, go to war, write a song, commit a crime, paint a work of art, join a cult, pursue a dream, take a leap of faith, and for me, to finish this book. In short, passion is what makes us care. And because we care, we are inspired and are able to inspire others. If students want to inspire their audience, they must convince them of their passion. They need to do this with more than just their words. It needs to be evident in every action they take on the stage.

> **TED TALK**
>
> *How to Speak So That People Want to Listen by Julian Treasure* is a TED Talk where the speaker gives all sorts of examples of how to show more expression in your words.

I talked in Chapter 8 about how you can be persuasive using a combination of logos, ethos, and pathos. In order to inspire, though, students definitely need to tap into the pathos region. The only way to inspire people is through their heart. There are several ways to do this, but five of the most powerful are:

- Tell personal stories
- Involve humor
- Deliver a strong, clear message repeated several times
- Show your passion
- Your non-verbals

Through a combination of personal stories, many of which are funny, having a strong clear message, being enthusiastic, and using her non-verbals effectively, she shows her passion and then some.

> **TED TALK**
>
> *Every Kid Needs a Champion by Rita Pierson* is a TED Talk where the speaker uses all five of these elements of passion.

Telling personal stories

Although talked about in an earlier chapter, personal stories are a very effective way to tap into the pathos of your audience. People care about stories. This is why film, television, and books are so popular. Most everyone loves a good story, especially one that moves them. This is what makes people care.

Although a brain expert, she actually uses her own personal story of having a stroke to accentuate her point.

> **TED TALK**
>
> *My Stroke of Insight by Jill Bolte Taylor* is a TED Talk that uses a personal story very well.

Students can use their own stories to tug at the heartstrings of an audience. Megan Washington is a professional singer who has a stutter. Singing is not a problem, speaking in public is a nightmare. And yet, she gets in front of an audience and tells her story. Through this personal story, the audience begins to think to itself, you know, if this woman can get in front of hundreds of people and make herself vulnerable, maybe it's not that big a deal to do it myself. It is most certainly inspiring.

Of course, students do not need to tell a tale of such woe in order to make a connection with the audience. But we all have stories that taught us lessons. Have students think about such

> **TED TALK**
>
> *Why I Live in Mortal Dread of Public Speaking by Megan Washington* is a TED Talk where the speaker uses her own story about being a stutterer.
>
> It is also a great video to show students about the fear of public speaking. It will certainly put things into perspective for them.

> **TED TALK**
>
> *I Got 99 Problems … Palsy is Just One by Maysoon Zayid* is a TED Talk that uses a lot of humor to inspire.

> **TED TALK**
>
> Here are two TED Talks that use humor well:
> *Do Schools Kill Creativity? By Sir Ken Robinson*
> *Inside the Mind of a Master Procrastinator by Tim Urban*
> Which one do you think used humor better?

stories in their lives and consider if the telling of one of these will help to support their throughline and, at the same time, connect them with their audience.

Involving humor

Another way to connect to an audience and show passion is through humor. I'm not sure what it is about humor, but it has a way of loosening an audience up and making a speaker someone they want to listen to. Take, for instance, this TED Talk:

The woman giving this speech has cerebral palsy. This talk could certainly have taken a more serious tone. Instead, she chose to make light of her situation until the audience is practically eating out of her hands.

When I say humor, I don't mean getting up there and telling random jokes. A speaker is not expected to be a stand-up comedian. I mean putting the audience in a position where they laugh while still retaining the integrity of the throughline.

Take, for instance, these two very famous TED Talks:

I show these two back to back to my students and ask them which one is funnier. This varies, probably split down the middle. However, when I ask them what the throughline of each of the talks was, almost no one can tell me that Ken Robinson is talking about creativity in schools. Yet everyone can tell me Tim Urban was talking about procrastination. Why is this the case? Because Tim Urban's humor has a direct connection to his throughline. Everything he says that is funny has to do with procrastination, whether it be the instant gratification monkey or the panic monster, to the stories he tells about him wasting time instead of doing what he is supposed to, like his senior thesis and preparing for the TED Talk itself. The audience is not laughing for the sake of laughing. They are laughing at his situation, and that situation is procrastination, the very focus of his talk.

Ken Robinson, on the other hand, tells some really funny stories, such as seeing a t-shirt that said, "If a man says something in the woods and there is no woman around, is he still wrong?" or that they were leaving England to get away from his son's new girlfriend. These are all very funny and get a great reaction from the audience, but they do not have anything to do with creativity. He does have some stories that do, such as Shakespeare as a child or the child drawing a picture of God, but lots of times the funny bits actually distract from the speech. Robinson himself has to use transitional phrases and words after getting a great reaction from the crowd to get them back on track.

If a student is going to use humor, it needs to support the throughline. A funny story, a humorous visual, or a joke should not be told unless it shows the point the speaker is trying to make or acts as an example.

Humor is certainly an excellent way to show passion, but you don't want people to forget the message as a result.

> **TED TALK**
>
> *The Clues to a Great Story by Andrew Stanton* is a TED Talk that tells a joke as its opening hook. However, it relates to his throughline of storytelling.
>
> ***DO NOT SHOW THIS TO STUDENTS. IT IS A VERY DIRTY JOKE***

> **TED TALK**
>
> *Why City Flags May Be the Worst-Designed Thing You've Never Noticed by Roman Mars* is a TED Talk that uses humor but never loses sight of the throughline.

Deliver a strong, clear message repeated several times

Martin Luther King Jr.'s *I have a dream* speech is mentioned in this book as being the high-water mark of public speaking. It is one of the most famous speeches in history, and the message is very clear, spoken in just four words: I have a dream. Not only does Dr. King say these words eight different times, but he brings them to life. He paints a clear picture of what his dream would look like: white and black children joining hands together, Mississippi transformed into an oasis of freedom and justice, where people will be judged by the content of their character rather than the color of their skin.

If students want to inspire an audience, having a memorable phrase that is repeated several times helps them digest it better. But it is more than that. It must also have some substance to back it up.

Being able to take your throughline and encapsulate it into a single, memorable sentence allows your audience to understand it better and recall it. Take this TED Talk, which boils a fairly complex idea into a single phrase, "the puzzle of motivation":

Remember, you should share just a single idea, but sometimes that can get lost in the shuffle of a 20-minute speech. Are you coming back to it constantly and consistently? Here is a TED Talk that repeats its catchy throughline several times:

Students will want to go back to their outline and make sure their throughline is repeated in each section of the speech: the beginning, each supporting point, and the conclusion. So a

> **TED TALK**
>
> *The Surprising Habits of Original Thinkers by Adam Grant* is a TED Talk that uses a clear throughline with stories to back up what it looks like.

> **TED TALK**
>
> *The Puzzle of Motivation by Dan Pink* is a TED Talk that uses a clear throughline from a fairly complex idea.
>
> Even though it seems to be about business, his throughline applies to many other things.

minimum of five times in the speech, but if it can be worked in more, all the better. Then they should check that they have stories and points that support this throughline and illustrate it for the audience.

> **TED TALK**
>
> *How Great Leaders Inspire Action by Simon Sinek* is a TED Talk that repeats his throughline of "people don't buy what you do, they buy why you do it".
>
> He repeats it seven different times, all as a coda to the stories he has told.

Show your passion

Passion goes a long way in inspiring an audience. I have said it before: if you act like you care deeply about what you are talking about, it is more likely that the audience will care as well. It should not be faked, though; audiences will see through that. Students need to be enthusiastic about what it is they are talking about. Audiences need to feel it as much as they are hearing it.

> **FOR PRACTICE**
>
> Challenge students to give mini-speeches on something they do not care about. See if they can express passion for it.
>   Some topics to consider:
> - The weather
> - The price of gas
> - The importance of math
> - Watching grass grow
> - Turning off the lights in your house to save energy
> - That boring book you read in English class
> - Socks
> - The value of good posture
> - Keeping your hedges trimmed
> - Paying taxes

A lot of this can be accomplished through non-verbals, which will be discussed in the next section. It is not just your voice that is excited, but your body as well. Look how excited this speaker

> **TED TALK**
>
> In this TED Talk, the speaker is very animated and expressive: *The Happy Secret to Better Work by Shawn Achor.*
>
> You cannot help but want to listen to his stories because he tells them with such glee.

> **TED TALK**
>
> In *The Transformative Power of Classical Music by Benjamin Zander*, the speaker obviously cares very deeply about classical music.
>
> He is so animated and enthusiastic about classical music that it sort of rubs off on you.

gets with his hands, even when not playing the piano, when he is talking about classical music:

The best way for a student to be passionate about his or her speech is to speak about something he or she feels passionate about. Seems simple, right? So let your students choose what they speak on. You can choose the purpose, but letting them choose the topic allows them to have a better chance of showing passion because presumably they will choose something they care about.

There are topics I need little motivation to be passionate about, with gifted education being the primary one. But I still have to make sure I show this passion to the audience. This comes through in my movement, the stories I tell, and the excitement in my voice when telling them.

Focusing on your non-verbals

The main things for students to consider are their voice and emotions. But they also need to consider the other ways they communicate with people, such as non-verbals. How are they using their hands? Are they making eye contact? Is their movement conveying passion? These little things put a speaker's words into action. A speaker can say she loves something, but if she delivers it with a monotone voice, looking away, and slouching her shoulders, it is going to be very difficult for the audience to believe her.

The three main focuses when it comes to non-verbals are:

1. Hands
2. Eyes
3. Movement

You will want to teach your students about each of these.

Hand gestures

Many people simply don't know what to do with their hands during a speech. They don't just want to let them hang from their shoulders, but they don't feel comfortable putting them in front of themselves. There are three cardinal sins you want to teach your students when it comes to hands. These can be printed out and given to students to remind them:

1) Don't put them into your pocket(s) – for some reason, this is a common place for people to put their hands. But it is like putting a muzzle on your non-verbals with your hands not able to express themselves.
2) Don't put them behind your back – kind of the same thing as in your pockets. It also puts you in a very passive position. When you are on stage, you want to be the dominant presence in the room, even with your body language.
3) Don't cover your mouth with them – you want to avoid stroking your face, resting one of your hands on your chin, or even placing it above your lip. All of these not only block your hands, they block your mouth.

You don't want anything getting in the way of your words and your audience, especially not yourself.

> **TODD TALK**
>
> To watch a video about what to do and not do with your hands that can be shown to students, go to:
>
> https://youtu.be/u95mOGAb4_4
>
>

Here are a couple of YouTube videos that can help your students with what to do with their hands:

Hands – *Best Hand Gestures For Public Speaking by BostonSpeaks* https://www.youtube.com/watch?v=f60IU-tQxMA

Gestures – *Gestures and Body Language by Toastmasters International* https://www.youtube.com/watch?v=-3ywrgCA-1I

When explaining hand gestures to students, have them visualize themselves as the director of a symphony. Their hands should reflect the rhythm of the speech. Just putting in random hand gestures that do not match what is being said can be distracting. They should not just do hand movements for the sake of doing something with them. Their movements need to have purpose; they need to intensify or accent an emotion. Have them find spots that are natural places to use these motions, such as when counting things off, when they are saying something with some emotion, or when they are coming to a climax on their point.

Eye contact

A speaker's eyes are the first means of connection to an audience. In a one-on-one conversation, a person wants to make eye contact with who he is talking with to show them he is paying attention and giving them his undivided attention. Students want to do the same thing with their audience, but there may be dozens or even hundreds of people in the room. They cannot possibly make eye contact with all of them. But they also don't want to stare off at nothing.

When I'm speaking to a room, I divide it into three parts: the middle, the right, and the left. I then work my way from section to section, not in a methodical way that seems patterned, but in a natural way. I find a person or group of people in each section and they are my points of contact. Or it may be an object such as a chair, a pillar in the room, or a table. One thing I also try to do is find my fan in the room. This is the person who is nodding to every point I am making or who is making eye contact with me. This allows me to connect with that person as well as boosts my confidence that what I am saying is landing with someone.

As much as possible, I am trying to make eye contact forward rather than back at my presentation slides.

What is the right amount of eye contact? Coach students that they don't want to verge on creepy eye contact, which is when they lock eyes with someone in such a way that it makes the person feel uncomfortable. It is more than a glance, though. The right amount is catching the eye long enough for the person to register you doing so. Three seconds is a suggested time for this if that is easier for students to figure out.

> **TODD TALK**
>
> To watch a video about proper eye contact that can be shown to students, go to:
> https://youtu.be/0KoWOWOBCJs
>
>

Movement

Many speeches are given with a person standing behind a podium, standing in one place. This is a big mistake. Movement on the stage brings another layer to a performance. I have been to many conferences, and I typically see three types of movers:

> *The Tree – this is the person who firmly stands rooted in one place. Because of this the audience is fixed on one spot and their eyes are not active. This can become very boring very quick. In*

addition this person may be behind a podium and you cannot see 90% of their body. Even if they were using hand gestures you wouldn't see them anyway. There is nothing wrong with this type of speaker, but if they are trying to get the audience inspired, their only weapon is their voice.

The Fan – this is the speaker who moves around the stage, usually in a smooth back and forth much like an oscillating fan. They go the left of the stage, speak for a little bit, and then move over to the right side. This is done in a very steady manner and the audience is able to follow this person easily. There are disadvantages and advantages such as there is a greater chance of not being lined up with the audience but there is easier access to body language.

The Rabbit – this is the speaker who is moving around the stage nearly the entire time, almost jumping from spot to spot. This can really get an audience going with the energy it brings and it is much easier to use some of the non-verbals. The drawback is that with such quickness this speaker can be difficult to follow. Sometimes they can enthuse a crowd, other times they can exhaust them. There is a fine line between.

One is not necessarily better than the other. It depends on the intent of the speech. If you are simply there to deliver information, the tree can be an effective way to go, especially if you have a slidedeck and do not want to be walking in front of it. If you are trying to get the audience excited about your topic, the rabbit can better help with that. Each has its advantages and drawbacks.

No matter which one of these a speaker decides to do, he needs to stand straight up and square to the audience. For the tree, this is easy because he has the podium lining him up. The fan has to make sure that every time he moves to one side or the other, he resets himself, shoulders square, body pointed toward the audience. Since the rabbit is always on the move, he has to reset after every movement. Here is a video of what this might look like:

Posture/movement – https://www.youtube.com/watch?v=m7SSj5Z5kTo

These non-verbals are so important not just for the audience but for the speaker as well. Standing in a confident manner gives one more confidence. Using hands to convey passion makes the speaker speak with more of it. Making eye contact with an enthusiastic audience member laughing at a story can encourage the speaker to be more humorous. Here is a TED Talk that explains just how important non-verbals can be, not just for the speaker mentally, but physically as well:

It actually has a hormonal effect, raising a speaker's testosterone and lowering cortisol.

Probably her most powerful words in this talk are "fake it till you make it". In other words, even if students are not confident, the lesson is to let non-verbals say otherwise. The audience won't know if someone is terrified inside if this is not shown on the outside.

> **TODD TALK**
>
> To watch a video about movement while speaking that can be shown to students, go to:
> https://youtu.be/aESqSgaKTNg
>
>

> **TED TALK**
>
> *Your Body Language May Shape Who You Are by Amy Cuddy*
>
> The speaker also does a great job of using body language well.

Shining a light

Remind your students, it is not just what you say, it is how you say it. Great speakers communicate what they want with their every move on the stage. It doesn't seem like much, but it really adds a lot.

These subtleties should not be tried in their very first speech, but rather added on like layers, which is why this book has students do a series of speeches. Once students have the voice down, they can work on where they stand. Once they have movement figured out, what are they going to do with their hands? All of these things combined help to show the passion that they have for their topic. It is this passion that sways an audience more than any words spoken. It is all about giving people a reason to listen.

When you put it all together, there are ten steps students can take to ensure an effective speech (Figure 10.1).

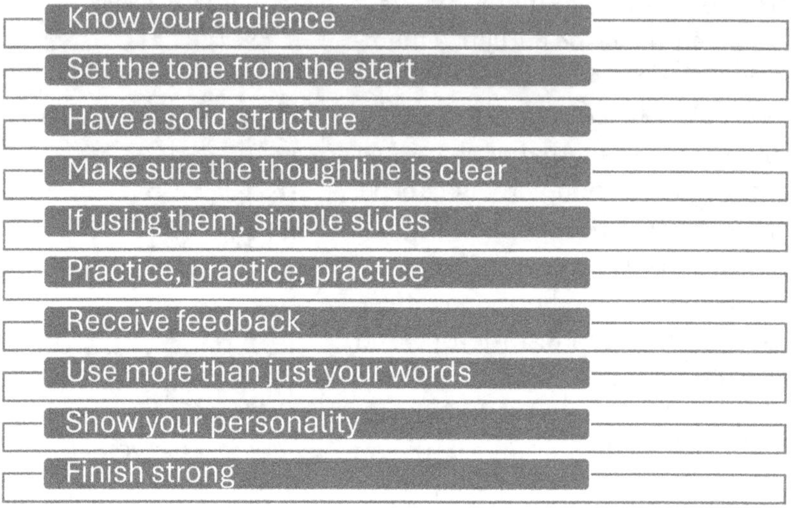

- Know your audience
- Set the tone from the start
- Have a solid structure
- Make sure the thoughline is clear
- If using them, simple slides
- Practice, practice, practice
- Receive feedback
- Use more than just your words
- Show your personality
- Finish strong

FIGURE 10.1

Conclusion

How students can continue to build their confidence in public speaking

The number one thing I want any student of mine to get from learning to publicly speak is the confidence to do so. Confidence is the great equalizer. With confidence, people believe. Without confidence, they doubt everything. But confidence is not something we can go to the store and purchase. It is not something that can be bestowed on someone. It is not even inherited genetically. Confidence must be earned.

So how do students earn it? There are three things that anyone can do in order to bolster their confidence when they have to speak in public:

> **TED TALK**
>
> *6 Tips for Building Your Confidence by Emily Jaenson* is a TED Talk that gives some advice on how to be more confident.

♦ Practice, practice, practice

Samuel Taylor Coleridge said, "He who is best prepared can best serve his moment of inspiration". This definitely applies to public speaking. Much like a sport, a musical instrument, or a hobby involving skill, one has to practice in order to get better. Part of what makes a person better is a familiarity with something, so there is more confidence in using it.

In regard to public speaking, when students practice their speech several times, they become more confident in the pronunciation, the delivery, the sequencing, and in how it lines up with the slide deck. When the student actually goes to give the speech, when she is trying to inspire an audience, she has the confidence to do so because she has familiarity with the words and she believes in what she is saying. It becomes a presentation rather than a reciting of the words.

- ◆ Be prepared

This goes hand in hand with practicing. Practicing allows one to be prepared, but there are additional things students can prepare to ensure that things go how they want them to. They have to control what they can control, and preparation is something they can definitely have a say in.

A list of some of the things they can prepare for is:

- ◆ If using technology, do you have it ready to go? I have three computer adapters with me because I find different venues have different hookups. Whatever can go wrong has gone wrong in regard to technology. I want to be prepared for anything.
- ◆ If you are using a slide deck, have it completed with a backup as well – I once got to a school and even with my three adapters couldn't connect my computer. Fortunately, I had a Google Slides backup and was able to use someone else's computer and present from that.
- ◆ Getting a good night's sleep – you want to be well-rested before your speech.
- ◆ Eating something before you present – you are going to be a little weak in the knees from nervousness. Getting breakfast or a good lunch before you speak, or some type of protein, ensures your body is fueled.
- ◆ How you react to your audience – you cannot control your audience's reactions, but you can control your reaction to their reactions. If the audience is lifeless or not giving you any signs on how things are going, just do your thing and don't worry about them.
- ◆ Prepare a goal – have a realistic goal set at the beginning of your speech. It might be something like managing your time, making eye contact, or trying not to go too fast. You know your tendencies and your weaknesses as a speaker.

Setting a goal helps you to prepare for these when they present themselves.
- Having tools in place to check for time – if you are giving a timed speech, is there a clock in the room you can refer to? Often, I will set the vibrating alarm on my Fitbit to go off when I just have a few minutes left. You can also ask a friend or moderator in the room to give you cues. As the teacher, I always give students a cue at halfway through, one for a minute left, and one for when time is up.
- Arrive early – nothing is less professional than being late to your own speech. Make sure you arrive well before the scheduled time, if there is one, and know where you are going.
- Doing your calming exercises beforehand – in our section on stage fright, there were several suggestions for ways to calm yourself down. Give yourself time and space to do these beforehand.
- Prepare for questions – this might not happen, but you want to be prepared in case it does. This requires anticipating what sort of questions an audience might ask and what your response might be. You may not be able to guess them all, but you will probably figure out the main ones.

The final thing students can do to gain confidence is to get experience. Like anything that is unfamiliar, they have to build this confidence. The first time someone drives a car, how confident do they feel? Are they ready to go on the freeway right away, or do they need to build up to that? Of course, once they have done it a few times, they can drive on the freeway without even thinking about it. Why is this? Because they have experience in doing so. They have built the confidence to deal with it. The same goes for public speaking.

- Experience

The only way students are going to continue to develop their public speaking skills is to actually publicly speak. This means finding as many opportunities to do so as possible. These can be very formal, such as the following:

- Running for student council
- Speech and Debate
- Model United Nations
- Mock Trial
- Toastmasters International
- Drama/theater
- Youth in Government
- TEDx

There are also more informal ways for students to develop their public speaking skills:

- Join a book club
- Work at a job where you speak to the public
- Volunteer when the teacher calls on people or asks for volunteers
- Do the announcements for your school
- Open mic night at the local coffee house
- Tutor other kids
- Speaking at a school board or city council meeting
- Special occasions such as weddings, graduations, or funerals

Not only that, everyday life presents people with all sorts of grand opportunities to gain experience speaking in public. Make sure students are looking for these and taking advantage of them:

- Talking with friends
- Ordering food
- Job interviews
- Class presentation
- Taking a phone call
- Supper time with the family
- Study group
- Playing on a team

These experiences are not going to fall into the laps of your students or be forced upon them. They will have to put themselves in situations where they will get to use their public speaking skills. This means having to get a little bit out of their comfort zone. But then, this is where the best learning takes place.

The final words you might want to leave your students with are that sometimes you have to fake it till you make it, as Amy Cuddy suggests in her TED Talk. Confidence is not about actually being confident, it is about conveying it even when you are anything but. If one acts confident, people will believe in you. And when they believe in you, you begin to believe in yourself.

> **TODD TALK**
>
> To watch a video of Verlin explaining how students can build their confidence, go to:
> https://youtu.be/JTF0b7OjpZg
>
>

Appendix

A list of all TED Talks mentioned in this book by chapter, as well as a list of TED Talks not mentioned but that would be good for students to watch and discuss can be found at:
https://www.thegiftedguy.com/public-speaking

The basic structure of preparing for any speech

1) Planning
2) Practice – time
3) Practice – content
4) Practice – effect
5) Present

Works cited

Black, P., & William, D. (2009). Developing the Theory of Formative Assessment. *Educational Assessment, Evaluation and Accountability*, 21, 5–31.

Dlugan, A. (2012). How to Use Rhetorical Questions in Your Speech. Six Minutes: Speaking and Presentation Skills, November 4.

Gallo, C. (2014). *Talk like TED: The 9 public speaking secrets of the world's top minds*. New York: St. Martin's Press.

Hattie, J. (2009). *Visible learning: A synthesis of over 800 meta-analyses related to achievement*. London: Routledge.

Marzano, R., Pickering, D., & Pollock, J. (2001). *Classroom instruction that works: Research-based strategies for increasing student achievement*. Alexandria, VA: Association for Supervision and Curriculum Development.

For Product Safety Concerns and Information please contact our EU representative GPSR@taylorandfrancis.com
Taylor & Francis Verlag GmbH, Kaufingerstraße 24, 80331 München, Germany

www.ingramcontent.com/pod-product-compliance
Lightning Source LLC
Chambersburg PA
CBHW070402240426
43661CB00056B/2505